Land of
Earth and Sky

A few speculative images
shyly define our place
trying to embrace our world
the necessarily outrageous flats
pitted against the huge sky

Peter Stevens

Land of
Earth and Sky
Landscape Painting of Western Canada

Ronald Rees

Western Producer Prairie Books
Saskatoon, Saskatchewan

For Diana

Printed and bound in Canada by
Modern Press ⟳ 1
Saskatoon, Saskatchewan

Cover & book design by John Luckhurst

The publisher acknowledges the support received for this publication from the Canada Council and Saskatchewan Arts Board.

Peter Stevens, ''Prairie: Time and Place'' from *Nothing but Spoons* (1969) is reprinted by permission of Delta Canada, Montreal. The poem was reprinted in *Twelve Prairie Poets*, ed. L. Ricou (Ottawa: Oberon Press).

Western Producer Prairie Books publications are produced and manufactured in the middle of western Canada by a unique publishing venture owned by a group of prairie farmers who are members of Saskatchewan Wheat Pool. From the first book in 1954, a reprint of a serial originally carried in the weekly newspaper, *The Western Producer*, to the book before you now, the tradition of providing enjoyable and informative reading for all Canadians is continued.

Canadian Cataloguing in Publication Data
Rees, Ronald, 1935–
     Land of earth and sky

Includes index.
Bibliography: p. 144
ISBN 0-88833-134-7

1. Landscape painting, Canadian — Prairie
Provinces.   2. Prairie Provinces in art.
3. Landscape painting — 20th century — Prairie
Provinces.   4. Landscape painting — 19th century —
Prairie Provinces.   I. Title.
ND1352.C2R43 1984   758'.1'09712   C84-091433-4

CONTENTS

ILLUSTRATIONS

ACKNOWLEDGMENTS

I would like to thank the Canada Council and the University of Saskatchewan for their support of the research on which this book is based. I am also greatly indebted to many librarians and archivists for their painstaking, and usually unsung, services; especially helpful were the staffs of the Public Archives of Canada, the Glenbow-Alberta Institute, and the Mendel Art Gallery, Saskatoon. I owe a particular debt of gratitude to Joan Steel, the Mendel Gallery's exemplary librarian.

INTRODUCTION

When staying at Moosomin, Assiniboia (now Saskatchewan) in 1896, Bertram Tennyson remarked that we see in nature whatever we bring eyes to see. Tennyson himself saw little in prairie nature and for the most part he was disappointed by what he saw. To paraphrase one of his verses, the blue of the prairie heaven wasn't as blue as the sea and the sward of the prairie landscape wasn't as green as England could be. Tennyson lacked the poetic gifts of his famous uncle—Poet Laureate Alfred Lord Tennyson—but he was astute. He recognized that his view of the landscape, like the views of other visitors to Western Canada in the nineteenth century, was conditioned by experience and culture. Life in England and a diet of English Romantic poetry and painting hadn't prepared him for an encounter with the austerities of a vast, dry, nearly featureless plain.

Tennyson's experience is instructive because all European views of Western Canada were conditioned by the backgrounds of the viewers and their expectations of the region. To some, the prairie was alien and threatening, to others it was romantically wild, and to yet others it was an Eden requiring only the ploughs of the settlers to stir it into productive life. The face of the prairie has changed since Europeans first saw it, but not so fundamentally as to explain the different ways in which it has been seen.

The landscape art of the prairies chronicles these changes in perception. Landscape paintings and drawings are charts of feeling and attitude as well as records of places. A painting tells as much about the painter and his times as it does about the places painted. How the prairie was seen depended on the temperament of the painter, on the landscape preferences of the period and, not least, on government policies toward the West. Once Britain and Canada had decided to promote settlement, the image of the West as a wilderness, that had served fur traders and adventurers, was replaced by one more likely to appeal to would-be settlers.

As well as being a landscape that Europeans found difficult to like, the prairie was a difficult landscape to paint. Because it fitted none of the scenic norms, there were no precedents for painters to follow. Over large areas, remarked a disgruntled corporal in the North West Mounted Police, no tree or bush relieved the aching eye while all around lay the dim, fading ring of the horizon. Without trees or hills to provide interest and shadow, and to lend depth to the scene, European painters were defeated. Even when the landscape did offer paintable objects these weren't the same as their cousins in Europe. Trees were small, thin, and without heavy swags of foliage; and standing water was more likely to be a brackish slough than a spring-fed lake. And everything, familiar and unfamiliar, was seen through the dry, clear, uncompromising prairie atmosphere. Colors tended to be stronger and edges harder than they were at home and, without humidity to soften and enchant, distance merely extended the view. To paint the prairie convincingly, Europeans had to adopt new techniques and work out new approaches.

Although landscape painting is its subject, this book is not, strictly speaking, an essay in art history. Paintings and drawings are treated as documents that elucidate the relationship of people to a land, not as objects for aesthetic appreciation. The emphasis is on culture, in the broad sense of the word, not on art. Also, because of the thematic structure of the book no attempt was made to treat prairie landscape painting comprehensively or to catalogue prairie painters. Only painters whose work is of historical interest, or whose vision affected ways in which the prairie was seen, have been included. As a result there are notable omissions that will be immediately apparent to readers familiar with prairie art.

Finally, a note on regional terminology. Because regions are defined by consensus not decree—political or academic—the vernacular is used throughout. "The West" or "Western Canada" refers to the flat, open country, drained by the Saskatchewan and Red Rivers, that lies between the Rockies and the Canadian Shield. British Columbia, in Western eyes at least, is west only in a geographical sense. Until settled by Europeans, the West consisted of two zones: a parkland of grasses and poplar bluffs that gave way in the drier south to treeless grassland. In line with popular usage, the term "prairie" or "prairies" designates both parkland and grasslands. Parkland and grasslands were specified only where distinction was necessary.

Art Before the Settlement

Likenesses of a New Land: *Topographers in the Canadian North West*

Until the middle of the nineteenth century Western Canada, then the Canadian North West, was virtually an unknown land. Separated from the nearest eastern colonies by a thousand-mile stretch of "immense marsh"—the Canadian Shield—it was, a spokesman for the Colonial Office remarked, "more difficult to reach than any existing colony of ours on the face of the globe." Until 1811, when Lord Selkirk persuaded a hapless group of Scottish highlanders to settle in the Red River, only fur traders had penetrated the region. Indeed, so fixed was the image of the North West as a permanent wilderness fit only for hunting and trapping, that Lord Selkirk's enterprise was seen as an impertinence: "one of the most gross impositions that was ever perpetrated on the British public," according to clergyman John Strachan of York (Toronto).

Although there were occasional lobbyists for agricultural settlement of the North West, most saw the region as a perpetual hinterland for the fur trade. David Thompson thought that it appeared to have been "given by Providence to the Red men forever," while the Governor of the Hudson's Bay Company, with one eye on the trials of the Selkirk settlers and another on securing the renewal of the company's lease of Rupert's Land, declared that the prairies and parklands west of Lake Superior were "not well adapted for settlement." As late as 1849 Parliamentary Under Secretary Ben Hawes ridiculed, in Westminster, the idea of settling such a "dreary territory" and asked if it was likely that any persons would go to such "barren tracts" when they had far more tempting lands to go to.

Apart from the length and severity of the winters, the region acquired a distinctly northern flavor from its domination by the fur trade and from the British fascination early in the nineteenth century with the search for a northwest passage through the Arctic Ocean. The typical fur brigade route ran through the southern fringes of the boreal forest so that on maps of the region, northern areas were shown in greater detail than southern. A northern cast also issued from the pens of travelers; a wilderness image gave their narratives a dramatic edge. Interested in the fur trade, Arctic exploration, or adventure, most travelers either ignored the parkland or, like Sir John Franklin, lumped the region with the Arctic or sub-Arctic. The grasslands, when considered at all, were dismissed as an extension of the Great American Desert and were considered useful only as a source of pemmican or as a buffer against the encroachment of American fur traders. Viewed either as the southern end of the sub-Arctic or the northern end of the Great American Desert, the Canadian North West was hardly alluring to settlers.

Although the North West was not, in the first half of the nineteenth century, of much interest to practical men there was much general interest in the region. For naturalists and ethnographers it promised new flora, fauna, and peoples, and for the less high-minded it offered vicarious adventure and romance. Imaginations enlarged by literacy and liberated by Romanticism were captivated by a region inhabited by only a scattering of Indians and half-breeds and a handful of whites. The variety and panache of early prairie society were caught in a letter by Lieutenant Blakiston, a member of the Palliser expedition, 1857:

> There is a little French Canadian who jabbers away in Normandy patois, broken English, and very indifferent Indian; then a stout looking Orkney man, whose native language being gaelic talks little better English than the others, knows also a little Indian, and few words of French; there are two . . . French half-breeds . . .; one is an old hand well up to prairie life, another a young careless lively talkative fellow, who having brought his fiddle with him, is ever straining away . . .; a fair haired Norwegian is among the party, and does the cooking for the postmaster an English half-breed and myself . . .; there is also a Cree Indian hunter and his squaw, an old Indian, a hanger on of the fort, who by the way is considered a great medicine man . . . The men wear entirely the moccasin, for a fact no other kind of shoe is to be got for love or money here.

Information about the North West came in the form of written accounts, maps, and pictures, the latter often illustrating reports and books of travel or, occasionally, published as a separate series. The pictures were vital because they compensated, as Captain Cook had recognized, for the "inevitable imperfections of written accounts." Europe had no buffalo, Indians or voyageurs, and English no words for a vast, empty plain or for such features as sloughs, coulees, or poplar bluffs. The old words—dale, lakelet, heath, meadow—didn't fit the new context. In new lands, as in no other settings, a picture was worth far more than the proverbial thousand words.

Most of the early pictures of the North West were pencil, ink, or watercolor sketches. Although the camera was available after 1851, it could not be considered a satisfactory field instrument until the end of the century. The photographer on Henry Youle Hind's Assiniboine and Saskatchewan Exploring Expedition, 1858, took very few photographs and most of these were of buildings and people in the Red River settlement. On the journey west of the Red River he appears to have taken only eight photographs and in these the landscape is blurred and distorted. Early cameras were best suited to portraits and close-up work and, because of the insensitivity of the plates, they could not photograph moving objects. Buffalo hunts, Indian dances, and thunderstorms—the best of the early West—were outside their range. Even stationary objects were difficult to photograph. The camera had to be set up and the plates sensitized, exposed, and developed on the spot. The process required from three to six hours of intensive labor and, because of the delicate chemistry of wetplate processing under field conditions, there was no guarantee of success. The final straw was the weight and bulk of the equipment: camera, lenses, tripods, trays, bottles, chemicals, and a portable darkroom weighed 500 pounds (226 kilograms). Sketching, by contrast, required only light and simple equipment and could be practiced in moments of leisure or during halts on the trail.

Until the development of an effective camera, the task of picture-making in the North West fell to the lowly topographer. Although he was sometimes accomplished, the topographer was a journeyman who was to painting what the taker of snapshots is to photography: a maker of likenesses or explanatory sketches, not an interpreter. His truth was factual, not imaginative, and it was, as Paul Duval has remarked, sometimes as empty of spirit as a mail order catalogue. Yet to Victorian audiences avid for information about new lands it was much prized. Anyone in the North West capable of making a pleasing sketch or writing a narrative was guaranteed an audience. So great was the demand for information that even painters with romantic inclinations were restrained by the greater need for documentation.

As amateurs for whom sketching was either a pastime or a mere adjunct to professional duties, the topographers came from many walks of life. A roster would have included military and police officers, surveyors and engineers, adventurers, tourists and early settlers. The largest single group were military officers who had either learned the rudiments of landscape sketching at their military academies or, if well-born, acquired them as part of the civilized accomplishments. Behind the academy-training lay the belief that by drawing the landscape, officer cadets would get to know it in a way that would have escaped casual observation. Instruction at the academies took the form of repeated lessons in technique that, once mastered, allowed recruits to limn the elements of any landscape. The drawing masters were often watercolorists who, by instructing at the academies, kept alive the centuries-old link between cartography and art. The first cartographers were landscape painters and the first maps bird's eye or panoramic views of landscape.

As well as being the most numerous group, military topographers were also the first to visit Western Canada. Franklin's party on his first Arctic expedition included two topographical surveyors, midshipmen George Back and Robert Hood. British Admiralty expeditions in the eighteenth and nineteenth centuries carried at least one graphic artist. Back accompanied Franklin on all three of his Arctic expeditions and his sketches were models for the aquatints used by Franklin to illustrate his narratives. The midshipmen's duties were to draw landscape and native peoples and to make scientific observations and maps. Virtually all of the maps and sketches made on the Franklin expeditions were of the Arctic and sub-Arctic, but a visit to Fort Carlton during the first expedition produced one of the earliest published drawings of the parkland. It was a crude but accurate drawing by Back of a buffalo pound in a landscape studded with the dark silhouettes of poplar bluffs. Back's drawing is nicely complemented by an entry in Hood's journal:

> When a large band of Indians is collected, the Buffalos are taken in a kind of pound, which is a circular space enclosed by stakes, having a narrow entrance at the edge of a declivity above the level of the pound. From the entrance two hedges of stakes gradually diverge to such a distance that the mouth of the road opens 2 or 3 miles. Some hunters on horseback drive a herd towards the opening and others conceal themselves behind the hedges. When the Buffalos begin to perceive the hedges on each side, the hunters stationed there rise and terrify them by shouts, so that they rush forward and precipitate each other down the declivity into the pound, where they are dispatched at leisure with spears and arrows.

A military reconnaissance, with less disinterested objectives than Franklin's, also occasioned the first sketches of the grasslands. Prompted by American territorial ambitions in the Pacific North West, summed up by President Polk's ringing slogan, "54°40' or Fight," the British government in 1845 dispatched lieutenants Henry James Warre and Mervyn Vavasour on a reconnaissance that took them across prairies and mountains to the disputed Oregon territory. Posing as tourists interested in hunting, wildlife, and scenery, Warre and Vavasour journeyed from Fort Garry to Fort Edmonton and then south to the Bow River and the grasslands before crossing the mountains.

The lieutenants' disguise allowed Warre to exercise his considerable talents as a watercolorist so that he returned to London with a portfolio of watercolor sketches as well as an official report. The sketches were eventually

H. J. Warre, *Buffalo Hunting on the Western Prairie*

reproduced as tinted lithographs and published as a series with text. Although on an official assignment, Warre could not contain his excitement in the landscape of the foothills, buffalo hunting, and the life of the Indians: "The excitement attendant upon the hunting of the buffalo must be enjoyed to be appreciated. Over hill and dale you follow on horseback, at full speed, . . . and fire only when sufficiently near to be certain of your mark." And: "I can imagine nothing more picturesque and more perfectly graceful than a Blackfoot Indian in his war costume, decorated with paint and feathers, floating wildly in the wind, as he caracolles on his small but wonderfully active barb, in the full confidence of his glorious liberty." But Warre's enthusiasm for the western scene did not include the very stage on which much of it was played, the grasslands. He dismissed these as an irredeemable wasteland offering "little to attract the eye, or tempt the industry, of even the most industrious husbandman."

A military reconnaissance of a leisurely sort also produced two early views of Manitoba. Charles Adolphus Murray, the seventh Earl of Dunmore, was one of several young officers from Britain and the Continent to observe the Civil War in America. Murray traveled west at least as far as the Manitoba parkland; notes on the back of two delicate watercolors indicate that they were painted in "Prince Rupert's Land" or "Hudson's Bay Territory" in September 1862. The watercolors were skillful and sensitive, but the heavy massing of the foliage and the softness of the light were more suggestive of the British countryside than the Manitoba parkland.

Besides sending officers on reconnaissance duties, British and Canadian governments stationed troops at Fort Garry. On two occasions, from 1846 to 1848 and 1857 to 1861, a military presence was thought necessary to protect the North West from encroachment by Americans and to check the growing unrest among the Metis who, it was feared, might join the Americans in the event of an attack. But so anxious were America and Britain to avoid conflict that the North West was, in effect, a peacetime posting. The men, who disliked the country, were bored and desperate for amusement. In winter, according to one Hudson's Bay Company officer, they seemed to "fret in their cages like wild animals," and with the US border a tempting sixty miles away a few even deserted.

The lack of urgency in garrison life is reflected in the drawings of Captain George Finlay who was stationed at Fort Garry for the duration of the Oregon dispute. Most of the drawings of the garrison were made less with an eye to future defense than to the interest of the artist and to the instruction and amusement of friends and relatives at home. Finlay made cheerful sketches of the soldiers hunting and tobogganing, and drew bird's eye views of the Fort and the Red River settlement that have no apparent military purpose. Finlay also had ethnographic interests. He made sketches of the Eskimo and Indians and the general life of the settlement. His ethnographic interests were shared by Major George Seton. Seton was posted to Fort Garry in 1857 and the following year he was assigned to accompany the Assiniboine and Saskatchewan Exploring

George Seton, *Bison Americanus,* 1858

George E. Finlay, *Duck Hunters in Camp,* 1847

Expedition led by Henry Youle Hind. At Fort Garry and on the expedition west, Seton made detailed notes and sketches of Indian customs, ceremonies, and equipment.

Service with the North West Mounted Police undoubtedly was more demanding than garrison life but it, too, allowed ample time for sketching. The most accomplished police artist was R. B. Nevitt, a young assistant surgeon from Savannah, Georgia. On the force's founding march to the North West in 1874 Nevitt's lesser duties were to make meteorological observations, to study Indian dialects, and to record the plants and animals of the country through which he and his companions passed. On the march Nevitt was too busy tending to men suffering from dysentery and exposure to do much sketching and too overwhelmed by the landscape to have any taste for it. He found the prairie "a wild, wild region . . . desolate and barren, a very Sahara" that could make him feel "intensely lonely."

Only at the Souris River and in the Sweetgrass Hills, both of which he sketched, did his aversion to the landscape break down. At Fort McLeod, "a beautiful place in the valley of the rivers," he was much happier, and during his two and half years there the isolation and the relatively healthy condition of the men allowed him to sketch at will. He sketched the landscape, the Indians, the day-to-day life of the Fort, and he made drawings of Crowfoot, chief of the Blackfeet, and the legendary Jerry Potts, the half-breed police scout whose sense of direction was said to be proof against the strongest blizzard and the blackest night. Nevitt also made the first sketches of Forts Walsh, Kipp, and Calgary, and he kept a record of the significant events that he witnessed. Examples were the meeting at Fort Walsh between Major Irvine of the NWMP and Sitting Bull shortly after Sitting Bull's defeat of General Custer at Little Big Horn, and the signing of Treaty Number 7 at the Blackfoot Crossing of the Bow River. Nevitt's sketches of the treaty-signing ceremony and of the Indian and NWMP camps, were the only on-the-spot representations of the event. A number of Nevitt's sketches were reproduced in the *Canadian Illustrated News.*

Topographers also accompanied civilian expeditions to the North West. Surveyors and engineers, whose first duty on government expeditions was to make maps, usually had some training in drawing. Their sketches were used as a supplement to maps and as the basis for illustrations in published accounts of the expeditions. John Fleming's pencil sketches, made on the Assiniboine and Saskatchewan Expedition, were models for the twenty watercolors that illustrated the published account.

Preeminent among the surveyor/engineer artists was William Armstrong, an Irish railway engineer who for twenty years was drawing master at the Toronto Normal School. In 1870 Armstrong joined, as engineer and bridge builder, the Sir Garnet Wolsey Expedition sent out to suppress the Metis rebellion at Fort Garry. It was the first of several visits to the North West, during which Armstrong made sketches of the Indians and collected weapons, tools, and ornaments. Armstrong was an illustrator who had no compunction about using the work of other artists. Several of his watercolors were based on H. L. Hime's photographs and on the sketches of other topographers. It was, Armstrong intimated, cheaper to use them than to visit the actual places. The practice, which was general, suggests that the topographers' sketches were valued chiefly as items of information, not as objects of aesthetic interest.

Although most of the documentary sketching of the early West was done by officers and surveyors as an extension of their official duties, two of the most valuable single

William Armstrong, *Buffalo Meat Drying,* 1899

contributions came from civilians unconnected with the army, the NWMP, or government surveys. First on the scene was Peter Rindisbacher, a sixteen-year-old Swiss youth who came to the Red River colony in 1821 with 164 of his countrymen. Lured by advertisements that were "highly colored" and that led them to expect of the country "more than can be realized," the Swiss emigrants were Western Canada's first victims of blatantly misleading advertising. Through a misapprehension which Lord Selkirk's agents on the upper Rhine had not troubled to correct, the Swiss had thought they were bound for the Red River of Louisiana where they would find a warm climate and hospitable French-speakers. Instead they had to suffer bitter continental cold and the hostility of hunters and fur traders who did not take kindly to the arrival of a large group of intending farmers. For four of the five years that the Swiss stayed at Red River they were forced by poor harvests to winter on the buffalo plains where, unable to hunt themselves, they subsisted by serving the hunters. They were finally driven out of the Red River in 1826 by a disastrous flood and resettled south of the border in the Upper Mississippi Valley.

Rindisbacher's record of his Canadian sojourn began at York Factory on Hudson's Bay, where the Swiss landed. There and on the journey south he made drawings of the Eskimo. At Red River he sketched the buildings of the settlement and the life and labors of the Indians, Metis, and Europeans who lived in and around it. Rindisbacher found work as a clerk with the Hudson's Bay Company and his duties took him to Indian and Metis camps. His Indians were cardboard figures, smoothed out and posed in the stiff neo-classical manner, but in matters of clothing and equipment he was all eyes. Alvin Josephy, Rindisbacher's biographer, has painstakingly categorized the objects and activities documented in the paintings and drawings: the exact dress and ornaments of the Cree, Assiniboines, and Chippewans; trade goods used in barter with the Indians; the uses made of dogs; seasonal methods of hunting, fishing, and traveling; household arrangements within the teepees; the customs, dress, and equipment of the traders and settlers; the buildings of the settlement.

Rindisbacher's sketches were so vivid and appealing that they were sought after as souvenirs by agents and servants of the Colony and the Hudson's Bay Company. With an eye to future sales he made working drawings in pencil or ink and then made copies in watercolor, changing details to suit the needs of his clients. He used the drawings in much the same way as a photographer uses a good negative. An order, made through an accountant in Fort Garry, has survived:

The ones I should like to have in particular are—the Plain Indian on Horseback shooting an enemy—the Group of Indians where the scalp is introduced. Captain Bulger's palaver—the death of the buffalo and two or three buffalo pieces in which I think the lad excels—as also travelling in winter with an Indian guide before the sled—Of all these I have seen several different copies, so that I conclude he keeps one copy to take another from as occasion may require—A subject at which I have not as yet seen any attempt of his, and which I should like much to have is—Assiniboine stealing horses.

Some of the drawings that were taken to England were lithographed, bound, and sold to collectors.

Rindisbacher was a talented painter and his admirers may object to his designation as a topographer. But like all topographers he was interested in unusual objects, activities, and incidents, not in mood. Unfailingly cheerful and picturesque, his sketches gave no hint of the hardships suffered by his compatriots, nor of the precariousness of Red River which was then, as R. M. Ballantyne put it, "a spot on the moon . . . a solitary ship upon the ocean."

Peter Rindisbacher's only civilian rival as a chronicler of the details of frontier life was William G. R. Hind, brother to Henry Youle Hind, the well-known explorer and naturalist. A restless and eccentric Englishman, Hind joined in Toronto in 1862 a party of forty-four "Overlanders" bound for the Caribou goldfields of British Columbia via the old fur traders' route across the prairies and the mountains. The Overlanders traveled by train and steamer to Red River, by then a substantial settlement, where they bought oxen, horses, and Red River carts for the westward journey. The Metis still hunted the buffalo but in the Scots and English districts hayfields and fenced croplands stretched back from the houses along the river.

During the Overlanders' stay at Red River and on the journey west, Hind filled a large sketchbook with pencil drawings and watercolors. These were supplemented several years later when Hind wintered at Red River on his way back to Toronto. Hind's approach to his subjects and his technique made him an ideal reporter. He professed to have no interest in mood and atmosphere and when he was asked on an earlier expedition to Labrador if he could convey the sublimity of a scene that included ice-covered cliffs, rapids, and lightning, he replied: "You can paint the woods, the trees and the ice, but the radiance and light are beyond human art."

In England Hind had been instructed in the precise techniques of Pre-Raphaelite painting. Impatient with the emotionalism and impressionism of Romantic art, the Pre-Raphaelites returned to the punctiliousness of medieval painting as it had been practiced before the time of Raphael. An approach that stressed painstaking accuracy and the use of strong colors could hardly have been better suited to recording the fine detail of a new land or have been more consistent with the scientific character of the age. In Hind's painting of a duck-hunting party, for example, the ducks (mallards) and the flowers (wild blue Iris) can be identified, and in a sketch of a Metis repairing the wheel of a Red River cart details of clothing, tools, and construction methods—down to the distinctive zig-zag joints of the wheel rims—are set down accurately.

Although a trained and skillful painter, Hind was a reporter of the documentary or topographical school. In the main free of trends and fashions in art, the topographers felt no compulsion to compose or idealize their landscapes. They did not make an Eden of the prairie or noble savages of its inhabitants. Free of the visual stereotypes that were the stock-in-trade of most professional painters, they provided unaffected and informative views of a little-known land.

The West as Romantic Wilderness:
The Art of Paul Kane and Frederick Verner

In unfamiliar surroundings the initial impulse is to document and record. But new lands are doorways to more than new worlds of fact. The question—"what does this place look like?"—begs another: "What does it feel like to be in it?" In Henry Youle Hind's public account of the Canadian Red River Exploring Expedition, 1859, there is a watercolor sketch based on a photograph taken by Humphrey Lloyd Hime, the expedition photographer. The photograph is of a flat stretch of Red River lowland, west of Winnipeg. In the foreground of the photograph is a human skull. In Hind's sketch the skull is larger and more prominent, and the straight line of the horizon—the dominating feature of the photograph—has been washed out. With a few brush strokes Hind (or his surrogate) attempted to convert an awesome landscape into one that was conventionally threatening. By using the landscape as a vehicle for human emotion, Hind, the professional natural scientist, abandoned his role as objective reporter.

For Europeans, and Canadians and Americans in the settled East, the Canadian and American Wests were a rich source of new experiences and new sensations, even if most could enjoy them only at second hand. Europeans in particular thrilled to images of a vast, unspoiled wilderness conveyed, for example, in the books of James Fenimore Cooper and R. M. Ballantyne. William F. Butler, who was to write the nineteenth century's most popular book on the North West (*The Great Lone Land*, 1872), remarked that as a boy he had read the works of Fenimore Cooper with "an intensity of interest never to be known again." The Swiss painter Rudolf Kurz, who suffered from a malaise then common enough to be given a name, "Europamudigkeit" (weariness with Europe), was also spellbound by the New World: "From my earliest youth," he wrote, "primeval forest and Indians had an indescribable charm for me. In spare hours I read only those books that included descriptions and adventures of the new world. . . . I longed for unknown lands, where no demands of citizenship would involve me in the vortex of political agitations. I longed for the quietude . . . where neither climate, false modesty, nor fashion compels concealment of the noblest form in God's creation."

So alluring was the North West that by the middle of the century the Hudson's Bay Company found it necessary to withdraw its service as universal host west of Fort Garry. After 1845 travelers unconnected with the fur trade were charged a daily lodging fee of ten shillings. Among the travelers was Paul Kane, a young and then unknown painter from Toronto.

Born in Ireland in 1810, Kane came with his parents to Toronto while he was still a boy. He had some instruction in drawing at a local school and after working as a sign painter, furniture decorator, and portrait painter, he went to Italy in 1841 to study art. In the galleries of Rome, Venice, and Florence he copied the old masters, acquiring the academic experience then thought to be indispensable to a young painter. A prophetic visit to England in 1843 introduced him to the work of George Catlin who in that same year had reopened in London an exhibition of American Indian paintings. Besides seeing the paintings and meeting Catlin, Kane must also have read Catlin's book, then recently published. *Letters and Notes on the Manners, Customs, and Conditions of the North American Indians* (1841) was a record of Catlin's life with Great Plains tribes between the years 1830 and 1836.

Catlin's sympathetic view of the Indians struck a responsive chord in Kane and changed the direction of Kane's artistic interests from portrait painting. Kane left London determined to do as much for the Indians of the North West as Catlin had done for the Indians of the American Plains. In 1845 he set out from Toronto with "no companion but my portfolio and box of paints, my gun, and a stock of ammunition." He spent his first season with the Ojibway along the shore of the northern Great Lakes and the following spring he began a three-year odyssey that took him across plains and mountains to the Pacific coast. West of Fort Garry Kane traveled with the colorful fur brigades as a guest of the Hudson's Bay Company. Sir George Simpson, then Governor of the Company was one of Kane's sponsors.

Like Catlin, Kane was convinced that the Indians were doomed and he resolved to leave a record of their lands, customs, and chieftains. "The principal object of my undertaking," he noted, "was to sketch pictures of the principal chiefs, and their original costumes, to illustrate their manners and customs, and to represent the scenery of an almost unknown country." Kane worked constantly, and in his journal and portfolio of nearly five hundred sketches he compiled an unparalleled documentary record of the Plains and Pacific coast Indians. On the prairies he sketched Metis, Sioux, Saulteaux, Cree, Blackfeet, and Assiniboines, all phases of buffalo hunting, and all of the Company forts that he visited.

When he returned to Toronto in 1848, Kane embarked on his larger purpose which was to convert his field sketches, chiefly in pencil and watercolor, into finished canvases. His objective was to produce a cycle of one hundred paintings that would rival Catlin's Indian gallery. He completed the paintings in 1855 and for the next four years he worked on an illustrated account of his western travels. *Wanderings of an Artist among the Indians of North America*, which was obviously inspired by Catlin's book, was published in 1859. It, and several subsequent editions, sold out to an enthusiastic readership.

Paul Kane, *Half Breeds Running Buffalo*

Paul Kane, *A Prairie on Fire*

The contrast between the spontaneity of the sketches and the stiffness of the canvases is now a commonplace of Canadian art history. In the sketches the figures are natural, the skies clear, the colors convincingly bright and luminous, and the landscapes all of a piece. When Kane exhibited the sketches in Toronto an appreciative reviewer commended their honesty: "Nothing has been sacrificed to effect—no exaggerated examples of costumes—no incredible distortions of features are permitted to move our wonder of what is sufficiently wild and striking without improvements."

Little of the truthfulness of the sketches survived the passage through the studio. Once in his studio Kane was an academic painter, hostage to the conventions of art. The recognizable human Indians of the sketches were transformed in the studio paintings into the noble, and seemingly invulnerable savages of eighteenth-century neo-classical art. For effect, they were dressed in regalia selected from Kane's collection of Indian artifacts. Landscape fared no better than figures. Convention dictated that serious paintings must be sombre so the clear skies of the sketches were replaced in the canvases by cloudbanks and thunderheads. Contrast Kane's oil painting of Fort Edmonton with his watercolor sketch of the

same scene. Accuracy too was often sacrificed for effect. In the finished paintings the pale light of the moon or the red glow of a campfire frequently replaced natural sunlight. Reconstitutions of this kind transformed whole landscapes.

The contrast between the sketches and the finished paintings is so striking that critic Barry Lord has accused Kane of using the Indians as exotic subject matter for self-serving artistic ends. Charles W. Jefferys, the painter and illustrator, was more charitable. He saw Kane as a victim of time and place:

Trained abroad, he naturally adopted the European art traditions of his time. Consequently we see in his pictures of the North-West not the brilliant sunlight of the high prairie country and the foothills, not the pure intense colour of the north; we see instead the dull, brown tones of the studio and gallery picture of the Middle Europe of his day. The topography may be North American, but the atmosphere both physical and mental, which bathes the scene is essentially European. His Indians, though authentic and convincing in details of physiognomy and costume, are incongruously conventional in their actions and gestures, and in this respect resemble the poses of the models and the antique classical statues of the academic studios in which he learned his craft.

A quarter of a century earlier Nicholas Flood Davin noted the same characteristics:

> Though he studied our scenery and Indian customs at first hand, he did not wholly give himself up to nature. The Indian horses are Greek horses; the hills have much of the colour and form of those of Ruysdael and the early European landscape painters; the foregrounds have more of the characteristics of old pictures than of our out-of-doors. All this is more particularly true of his later work, when, instead of going to nature, he remained in his studio, and painted and repainted his early sketches.

The abrupt change, from a documentary to a romantic treatment of nature, when Kane moved from field to studio, may also be attributed to the demands and expectations of patrons and viewers. Sir George Simpson, governor of the Hudson's Bay Company, requested "buffalo hunts, Indian camps, councils, feasts, conjuring matches, dances, warlike exhibitions, or any other piece of savage life that you may consider to be most attractive or interesting." Moreover, a public conditioned for over half a century to see Indians as the antithesis of moribund, civilized man, would have been disinclined to embrace more lifelike images. In the customary stereotypes, Indians were presented as models of fine feeling at one extreme and as gloriously impassioned savages at the other. They were idealized, emblematic figures on which Europeans hung their cultural and aesthetic predilections, not sentient human beings. That the Indians were thought to be threatened with extinction made them even more attractive. The comfortable melancholy induced by reflection on death and decay was central to the Romantic sensibility. Had there been genuine sympathy for the Indians, the misfortunes that befell them in the second half of the century would have caused an uproar.

In the last third of the century, the mantle of Indian painter that Kane had worn unchallenged for thirty years fell on Frederick Arthur Verner. A native of the village of Sheridan near Toronto, Verner as a boy had idolized Kane. Legend has it that he once knocked on the door of Kane's studio to ask for painting lessons only to have the door opened a crack, then closed in his face. Later the two became friends and Verner painted what is today the best-known portrait of Kane.

Like Kane, Verner was European-trained. He went to London in 1856 to study art in the city's schools, galleries, and museums. He returned to Canada in 1861 and the following year he traveled west through Ojibway country to Fort Garry and the Nelson River. Subsequent journeys in 1870 and 1873 took him across prairies and mountains to the Pacific coast. He traveled by canoe, horseback, and Red River cart and, like Kane, he compiled a portfolio of pencil and watercolor sketches that he later used as models for finished oils. By the mid-seventies Verner was a known and successful "western" painter. The *Canadian Illustrated News* observed in 1873 that he had "hit upon a very popular vein" and reported that most of the paintings in Verner's first exhibition with the Ontario Society of Artists had been sold. But in Canada the Indian's star was well past its apogee; one reporter noted darkly that Mr. Verner's devotion to the Red men was becoming tiresome.

Verner's paintings also attracted attention abroad. Verner settled in England in 1880 and in the following decade he exhibited frequently at the Royal Academy. In its review of the Academy's 1882 exhibition, the *Times* noted approvingly that since Catlin's time "nothing of equal interest has been exhibited to the English public." Verner's North West of the Indians and the buffalo, was the one which the English wanted. But where Kane's paintings had celebrated the pride and independence of the Indians, Verner's were elegiac. By the 1870s no sensitive observer could have been indifferent to the plight of the Indians, or, of their mainstay, the buffalo. Verner's buffalo were "The Fading Race" and his Indians, in contrast to the confident warriors of Kane's finished work, were shy and vulnerable.

Yet like all his western subjects, Verner's Indians were the product of a Europeanized, London-trained sensibility. His vision of the West, like Kane's, was romantic. In the paintings birch bark canoes emerge romantically from the mists, campfires glow in soft, evening light, and buffalo graze against backgrounds reminiscent of Scottish moors. The characteristic colors are brown, green, buff, and mauve. In short, Verner was in thrall to the old, wilderness image of the West which he continued to paint long after events had made it obsolete. For this he was chided as late as 1908 by the editor of the Toronto *Globe* who wrote that, while Verner's canvases might have had the charm of complete novelty for his English patrons, they represented the Canada of the past and not the Canada of the railway builder, the settler, the woodsman, and the miner.

The West as a Frontier of Settlement:
Special Artists for the Illustrated Press

In Canada, particularly, the image of the North West as a wilderness had begun to lose its appeal by the middle of the nineteenth century. Fear of American encroachment, the need for a bridge between Ontario and British Columbia, and the shortage of cheap land in Ontario prompted speculation about the possiblity of settling the North West. If Canada were to continue to attract immigrants from Europe and prevent its own population from emigrating to the United States, it had to be able to offer good land at nominal prices. Threatened with physical and economic confinement, Canadians looked beyond the barren Pre-Cambrian Shield, which stood like a portcullis on their own frontier, to the empty lands of the North West.

The old image of the North West as a wilderness fit only for buffalo, fur traders, and Indians no longer served the new interests. To meet the new expectations, the North West had to be reassessed. Expeditions dispatched after 1850 were required to look for transcontinental railway routes and to assess the resources of the region with an eye to its future settlement by farmers. Inevitably, as historian Doug Owram has remarked, the questions asked altered the conclusions reached. The Palliser and Hind-Dawson expeditions of 1857 and 1858 both found in favor of settlement and in doing so permanently altered perceptions of the region. By staying south of the fifty-forth parallel they severed the North West from its associations with the Arctic and sub-Arctic and by introducing the notion of a fertile belt—the parkland—they opened doors to the possibility of agricultural settlement. Later surveys were to open them still wider by extending the limits of the fertile belt to include the grasslands.

Reassessments of the North West were not restricted to the physical environment. Views of customary ways of life also changed. After

1860 hunting and trapping, once revered as the apotheosis of romantic freedom, fell from grace and the reputations of their practitioners suffered. Admired earlier for their generosity and carefree spirit, the Metis were vilified as "shiftless gypsies" for resisting the wholly settled life. Even more precipitous was the fall of the Indians. By the end of the century, the noble and independent savage of European fancy was a "dusky lounger" cluttering city sidewalks, and an importunate beggar seeking handouts on CPR trains.

To replace hunting and gathering with settled ways of life, the Dominion Government and the CPR solicited immigrants. The CPR opened its own immigration department in 1883, with the head office in London. To advertise the North West, paintings and photographs were displayed in government and CPR offices, and newspapers and magazines in eastern North America, Britain, and the Continent were bombarded with promotional material, both written and pictorial. The objectives were to efface the wilderness image of the North West and advertise the region's productive capacity. In print the tactic was to alternate hyperbole and restraint. Grasses were "wonderfully nutritious" and crops "splendid" but descriptions of landscape, which until then had rung the changes of the vocabulary of the sublime, were couched in homely adjectives: "It is a nice prairie covered with beautiful grass and dotted here and there with little poplar forests, which give the whole a very romantic appearance. The settlers whom we visited look forward to a very happy and contented future." Paintings and drawings substantiated the written reports. The prairie was seldom empty and it was always productive. A popular vehicle for demonstrating the productivity and attractiveness of farm life was a sequence of five or six annual pictures. In a typical run the farm progressed from a primitive shanty on unimproved land to a substantial frame house surrounded by a shelter-belt and a pattern of fields.

As well as producing its own copy, the CPR invited journalists to the North West, providing them with rail passes and accommodation at stopping points along the way. Particularly sought-after were the artist-reporters or "specials" of the illustrated press. Appealing pictures, as the CPR and the specials themselves well realized, were the most effective form of advertisement. "Sketches," noted Sydney Prior Hall of the *Graphic,* "set a person to thinking and they might convey ideas which written description would not, and prompt people to become better acquainted with the country."

As forerunners of today's photo-journalists, the specials were a new breed of artist. They had to be able to make quick, eye-catching sketches and, if necessary, supplement them with readable commentary. Like the topographers they worked with meager materials, often under difficult conditions. But unlike the topographers they were all trained artists and many had been schooled in the precise Pre-Raphaelite methods. Vague, romantic images might satisfy armchair travelers and adventurers, but newsreaders demanded accuracy. Potential investors and intending emigrants needed to know if a new land held out reasonable prospects for profit and a successful life.

The dominant theme of the sketches and reports was the civilizing of the North Western wilderness by a predominantly Anglo-Saxon society. England, as the Dominion Department of Agriculture declaimed, was the "great civilizer" and the "mighty colonizer" of the world. As products of middle-class English backgrounds and employees of an imperialist press, the specials worked within a context of unquestioned Anglo-Saxon superiority. Yet many of them had misgivings about the effects of colonization upon the Indians. William Simpson of the *Illustrated London News,* who had seen American Indians herded into reservations, thought they had been "cruelly wronged," while Arthur Boyd Houghton of the *Graphic* noted that European colonization meant "destruction to the men who live by the chase." The specials also had some feeling for emigrants who would give up home and country for life in a new, raw land. As guests of the railway and reporters for imperialist newspapers and magazines, the specials were indirect agents of the settlement, yet from time to time they conveyed a sense of the immensity of the prairie and the inherent loneliness of pioneer life.

But neither the times nor the circumstances of the specials favored a comprehensive or an objective view of the North West. If they traveled by train their path was "arrowy" and their accommodation luxurious. The North West as seen through a train window was hardly the North West of ordinary experience. J. G. Donkin, a sometime corporal with the NWMP, and a rare sceptic in the North West of the 1880s, opened his own account of the region with a dismissive commentary on the opposition:

> These [journalistic globe-trotters] are billeted in luxurious Pullman cars; the perfect service of the dining car causes all outward things to be suffused with a rosy light, and unbounded courtesy meets them at every turn. There are even bathrooms on these trains, and whenever the illustrious stranger pleases to alight at any of the mushroom prairie cities, every official connected with the immense bureaucracy which governs the North-West Territory hastens to do him honour, and act as his cicerone. So after having been transported across these limitless plains in palaces on bogies, and having been feted at every halting-place en route, they hie them back and add their testimony to the magnificence of the country. No one blames their public-spirited gratitude; but they have seen nothing of what lies behind the scenes, and they really know nothing of the vast stretch of wild and lonesome land beyond. ... Yet many of these invited travellers, after their arrowy flight, send forth their impressions of the unknown with ... much dynamic assertion.

Once the building of the railway had been decided upon and settlement became a certainty, the North West was seldom free of observers and reporters. The best-known, however, tend to be associated with particular incidents and with particular touring parties. First on the scene was Henri Julien of the *Canadian Illustrated News* whose subject was not the settlement but the measure that would ensure its orderliness: the now-famous march west, in 1874, of 275 officers and men of the North West Mounted Police. Keen to promote the new force, Commissioner G. A. French invited the *Canadian Illustrated News* to send an artist-reporter to record its dramatic infancy.

The march began in Fargo, North Dakota, the nearest rail point to the Canadian North West. Julien responded to the sight of open, treeless prairie with sentiments worthy of Captain Butler, on whose recommendation the force had been organized: "This narrow strip of planking (the station platform) was the dividing line between civilization and the wilderness. Behind us lay the works of man, with their noises; before us stretched out the handiwork of God, with its eternal solitudes. The first sight of the prairie is as impressive as the first sight of the sea. There, at our feet, it spread out, silent, immeasurable, sublime.

On the march west, Julien, then a young man of twenty-two, was more interested in the adventure of the journey, and the hazards attending it, than in what it portended for the future of the North West. Julien commented on the voracity of the blackflies and mosquitoes, the size of the hailstones, "nearly as large as walnuts," the grandeur of the prairie fires, and the disconcerting ease with which men could get lost on the open prairie. At the Souris River, where there was wood and water, he thought the country wonderful and waxed eloquent about its prospects. But farther west, as the country became drier and poorer, and as the marchers tired, his enthusiasm waned: "Not one green bush of the most dwarfish size to relieve the eye. The effect of this loneliness upon the imagination is very singular. The eye dwells on vacancy, tired of glancing at the blue sky above or the brown earth beneath. A feeling of weariness creeps over you, interrupted at intervals by vague longings for something beyond the far, low line of the horizon, which is ever barred across your vision." And on their arrival at the South Saskatchewan River, near Medicine Hat, the marchers found not "the perfect garden of Eden" as they had been led to expect, but land that was "little better than a desert." Grass and water were both bad, and for tea the men had to make do with "liquid mud." Even the Indians were disappointing. "In vain do you look for the type of a Pontiac or an Uncas. Still less are you blessed to behold a Pocohontas or a Minnehaha."

The artist-reporters who followed Julien came not on an adventure but to report on the prospects of the North West. They were more positive. Most were attached to promotional tours led by governors general. The most celebrated tour, and the best attended, was the Marquis of Lorne's. As both governor-general of Canada and son-in-law to Queen Victoria,

he was a willing instrument of British and Canadian policies. Disturbed by slow rates of immigration, the approach of American settlement, and the coolness of the British press toward Canada, the CPR and the British prime minister, Benjamin Disraeli, concluded that the best remedy would be a well-advertised tour by the young and attractive governor-general. Arranged for the summer and fall of 1881, it was attended by journalists from England, Scotland, France, and Canada. Among them was an artist-reporter, Sydney Prior Hall of the London Graphic, invited personally by the governor-general.

The vice-regal party traveled by rail to Portage la Prairie, then the "end of the steel," and westward from Portage by a variety of horse-drawn vehicles. The party was escorted by a detachment of North West Mounted Police and, by a supreme irony, the Cree chieftain Poundmaker, who served as guide on the Battleford-Edmonton leg of the tour. Four years later Poundmaker would join forces with Louis Riel, the Metis leader, to resist European settlement of Indian and Metis lands. On the tour Poundmaker was noticeably hostile to "the Great Brother-in-Law," as he called Lord Lorne.

Hall's sketches appeared almost weekly in the Graphic between August 1881 and December 1882 and they were frequently carried by the Toronto Globe and Mail. Images of desolation occasionally intruded themselves in [View of the Prairies], for example, but the drawings were more characteristically cheerful and lively and they fulfilled, without deliberate misrepresentation, the tour's purpose of creating a less forbidding image of the North West. Even so, they failed to satisfy the exacting editor of the Manitoba Free Press who complained that "Mr. Hall has confined himself too much to sketching Indian pow-wows." In Britain, where the wilderness image of the

North West was still popular, Indians were very good copy.

Hall was not noticeably sympathetic to the Indians, but his drawings chronicled a further stage in their decline. By 1881 they seemed to be in perilous condition. The buffalo had disappeared and the Indians, now confined to reserves, lived in such abject poverty that Lord Lorne was forced to remark that "in view of their starving condition, it was amazing how well we got on with them." He thought the Indians were doomed and predicted that within a few years the only survivors would be in the far north.

The plight of the Indians was the occasion for a pow-wow between the Blackfeet and the governor-general at Blackfoot Crossing on the Bow River. Hall's sketch of the pow-wow served as the model for an oil painting commissioned later by Lord Lorne. The pow-wow was a symbolic confrontation between vanquished and victors, the lowly and the lordly. Uniformed and authoritative, members of the vice-regal party sat on chairs or stood beneath an awning protecting them from wind and sun. Across from them, the bedraggled Indians sat on open ground around their chief, Crowfoot, who held up an empty flour cup as a symbolic gesture of the tribe's hunger and

S. P. Hall, [Conference at Blackfoot Crossing], 1881

the inadequacy of government rations. In the oil painting the Indians are neatly clad and well-fleshed, and the flour cup has been left out.

The Reverend James D. McGregor, representing the *Scotsman* and the *Edinburgh Courant*, described the scene:

I have rarely seen a more touching sight than the poor, infirm chief, with his finely chiselled countenance and bright smile as, leaning on his staff, and worse clad than any of his followers, he moved forward to his place; the shabby clothes, which the poorest artisan would be ashamed to wear, contrasting sadly with the Victoria medal which he wore on his breast. . . . It was touching, too, to hear the earnest way in which he pled for greater help from the Government for his starving people.

The reporter from the Toronto *Globe*, on the other hand, was unmoved. "The average chief," he wrote, "embodies so much utterly uninteresting verbous nonsense in the introduction to his speech that it is very tedious to listen to."

Before and after the pow-wows the Indians usually staged races, sham battles, and cere-

S. P. Hall, *Pow-wow at Blackfoot Crossing*, 1881

monial dances, chiefly for the entertainment of the visiting dignitaries. Hall sketched them lightheartedly: reverence for things aboriginal had given way to raillery. At Fort Qu'Appelle, where the Sioux gave a performance of the buffalo dance, he noted that the buffalo heads had painted, wooden horns. "Poor Sioux!" he wrote off-handedly, "Not a buffalo has been sighted for four years."

The vice-regal party and the attending journalists sang choruses of praise for the agricultural potential of the North West that might have been composed by Disraeli and the CPR. No voice rose higher than Lord Lorne's. He made an occasional reference to the disturbing immensity of the land, and to the prevalence of mosquitoes, but these were trifling disadvantages when weighed against the productivity and the picturesqueness of the fertile belt. His finest encomium was couched in verse.

Away to the West! Westward ho! Westward ho!
Where over the prairies the summer winds blow.

The West for you, boys! where God has made room
For field and for city, for plough and for loom.
The West for you, girls! for our Canada deems
Love's home better luck than a gold-seeker's dreams.
Away! and your children shall bless you, for they
Shall rule o'er a land fairer than Cathay.

In spite of Lord Lorne's blandishments, the North West failed to attract the expected number of British settlers. Emigrants continued to prefer America to Canada and in the late 1880s a shrinking wheat market reduced still further the attractiveness of the North West. With CPR stocks falling on the London exchanges, the time was ripe for another vice-regal visit. Lord Lorne's successor, Lord Stanley of Preston, was equally amenable to the idea of a western tour.

Lord Stanley's party traveled by special train from Quebec to Vancouver in September and October in 1889. In the party was Frederick Villiers, artist-reporter for the *Graphic*. The first prairie halt was at Winnipeg, then the "bull's eye city" of the North West, where they were greeted by a crowd of ebullient and staunchly Anglo-Saxon "Canada Firsters." "Though it was pouring with rain, and the streets were a foot thick with the tenacious Winnipeg mud," Villiers reported, "a torchlight procession, in which the whole populace seemed to join, surged around the

S. P. Hall, *Sioux Buffalo Dance,* 1881

Vice-Regal carriage en route to Government House."

After leaving Winnipeg, the party visited the new crofter settlement at Saltcoats where forty-nine Scottish families were busily preparing for "the cold snap," the women weaving warm clothing and the men sealing the walls of their log cabins with mud. Villiers drew a cheerful sketch of a crofter and his wife but Lady Stanley, in the privacy of her diary, recorded a different impression: "Oh! such a dirty, miserable house—making Prairie life not appear at all attractive." She preferred visits to Indian reserves where there were at least the trappings of a romantic past. She was dismayed at the sight of Indians in double-breasted suits, top hats, and gaiters but those

Frederick Villiers, *Home for the First Year in the New West*, 1889

who appeared in war paint and war dress, "shooting and yelling and firing their guns," provided the ultimate thrill of the tour. On the reserve at Gleichen, Alberta, she met Crowfoot—wearing a scarlet coat, buckskin breeches, and a shirt, and a huge treaty medal—and thought him "a very fine old man." Crowfoot was fifty-nine.

At Gleichen, Villiers made a sketch of Lady Stanley "fixing" a war-dance with a newly acquired Kodak and he observed, prophetically, that she made excellent photographs of the tour. The Kodak box camera was available after 1888 and was immediately popular with tourists. It was soon to be popular with artist-reporters. Villiers was the last special to accompany a vice-regal tour of the North West even though the tours continued into this century. Villiers crossed Canada again in 1894, but on that occasion he relied more on his Kodak than on his pencil.

It was fitting perhaps that the last of the old North West should have been recorded by artists who were themselves on the brink of obsolescence. The reign of the specials was brief but it spanned that critical phase in the history of the North West when the world of the Indian and the Metis was about to collapse

Frederick Villiers, *Lady Constance and Lady Alice "Fixing" a War Dance*, 1889

Charles Edwin Fripp, *The Dying North-West,* 1889

Charles Edwin Fripp, *The New North-West,* 1889

under the advancing wave of European civilization. The tragedy of the moment was caught by Charles Edwin Fripp when reporting for the *Graphic* along the line of the newly completed CPR in 1889. Fripp made a pair of sketches, one of an Indian, the other of a newly installed rancher. The Indian is a study in submission; huddled, withdrawn, and bewildered, he looks onto a world that he no longer understands. The rancher on the other hand is the embodiment of wilful confidence, rifle at the ready, stance upright and unyielding, eyes fixed firmly on the future.

Illustrated Books

In its efforts to promote the North West, the CPR was supported by public-spirited individuals who, in published letters, articles, and illustrated books, played fife to the CPR's drum. No author was more fervent than George M. Grant, recording secretary to the Sandford Fleming Expedition that set out in 1871 to determine a route for the proposed transcontinental railway. Using notes made on the expedition, Grant wrote *Ocean to Ocean* to stimulate immigration to Canada. Published in

1873, it was illustrated with engravings based on photographs taken during the expedition. *Picturesque Canada*, illustrated by the drawings of F. B. Schell, followed in 1882.

Ocean to Ocean, which was published within a year of Butler's *The Great Lone Land*, was a watershed in the history of perceptions of the North West. Although Butler was engaged on reconnaissance work for the Canadian Government, he directed his book, the last major celebration of the North West as wilderness, at "prisoners of civilization." *Ocean to Ocean* was an attempt to domesticate the North West. Descriptions of landscape revealed picturesque enclosures not sublime panoramas. "Everywhere," Grant wrote of the Touchwood Hills, "are grassy or wooded, rounded knolls, enclosing natural fields or farms, with small ponds in the windings and larger ones in the lowest hollows." And of the country along the North Saskatchewan River: "a lovely country, well-wooded, abounding in lakelets, swelling into softly-rounded knolls, and occasionally opening out into a wide and fair landscape . . . We were . . . in a country that could easily be converted into an earthly paradise." Its most serious disadvantage was the excessive richness of the soil, which produced straw in such abundance that it was difficult to get rid of.

Ocean to Ocean also represented a changed aesthetic. For Butler, the beauty of the North West lay in its uncontrolled immensity; for Grant, the appeal lay in its utility. Grant's appreciation of the landscape was inseparable from conceptions of wealth, fertility, and opportunity. In essence, it was a return to a pre-Romantic appreciation of nature when, as Ruskin put it, man enjoyed looking only at "the available and the useful." Grant's assessment of the North West was a catalogue of material riches: "It is a fair land, rich in furs and fish, in treasures of the forest, the field, and the mine; seamed by navigable rivers interlaced by swelling uplands, wooded hillsides, and bold ridges."

Picturesque Canada, published in 1882, simply extended the Arcadian vision. Thanks to John Macoun's recent delivery of the grasslands from semi-aridity, the entire region, Grant asserted, could now be proclaimed the "garden of the world." In 1880 Macoun, the Dominion government botanist, had been asked to make a further assessment of the grasslands, considered by Palliser and others to be too dry for cultivation. In a report that quickly became a standard part of Canadian scientific and popular thought, Macoun renounced previous opinion and declared that they could be farmed.

F. B. Schell, *A Prairie Stream*, 1882

24

Schell's drawings, which illustrated *Picturesque Canada*, promoted the garden image. They showed wooded stream courses and settled, productive landscape; picture space that might otherwise have been empty was taken up with disproportionately large clumps of grasses and flowers. In Manitoba, where most of the prairie drawings were made, the garden image had a ready-made vehicle in the Mennonite village settlements. Picturesque houses uncharacteristically—in the prairie context—clustered, windmills, traditional European dress, and herds of cattle gave the lie to the Butlerian conception of the North West as a great lone land.

A more objective and balanced assessment of the North West came from the pen of author/artist Edward Roper who wrote travel

F. B. Schell, *A Prairie Farmstead,* 1882

books on Canada and Australia. Roper was also a keen naturalist who collected samples of flowers, beetles, butterflies, and moths. He crossed Canada by CPR in 1887 and recorded his impressions in *By Track and Trail.* A keen imperialist, he lectured on his return to England (under such titles as "What does it Mean to Emigrate?") and exhibited oils and watercolors of Western Canadian life.

Like many professional writers and journalists, Roper was keenly aware of his responsibilities to intending emigrants. He warned that prosperity could be acquired only at the cost of immediate loneliness and that for every successful settler there was another who

F. B. Schell, *The Harvester,* 1882

F. B. Schell, *A Mennonite Village,* 1882

F. B. Schell, *The Virgin Prairie,* 1882

succumbed to the summer heat, the awful winter cold, and mosquitoes. The complaints of one English emigrant he interviewed amounted to a litany of despair: "The loneliness, the utter want of congenial society, the roughness, the immense distances, and the prospect of a dreadful winter."

Like most observers, Roper drew a sharp contrast between the parkland and the grasslands. The aspen bluffs of the parkland gave the land "a homelike, if not a picturesque look" even though the prevailing feeling was still one of loneliness. The grasslands he found desolate: "We passed a very few settlers' places (near Broadview, Saskatchewan), a hut or two of lumber, cold, bare, bleak in the extreme—no trees, no gardens, no fences, no roads . . . Loneliness, utter loneliness."

Roper's paintings, however, failed to convey the sense of desolation that he sometimes felt. Most are positive, even picturesque. He concentrated on the improved, not the primitive landscape, painting farmsteads and ploughed fields, chiefly in the parkland. His vision of the settlement was the then common one of a plain divided into regular fenced fields and covered with a heavy sprinkling of trees and farmsteads. Roper's one painting of the open prairie shows not "the most monotonous country" but a solid farmstead, flying a Union Jack. With brush in hand, Roper was very much the positive imperialist, and in one case he admitted to making "the most picturesque sketch possible."

The Art of the Settlement

Early Resident Painters: *The West through English Eyes*

Paintings and drawings of the West made before the settlement were intended for audiences in Europe and eastern North America and they were designed to inform and excite the romantic imagination. As settlers replaced trappers and traders an art that was primarily documentary gradually gave way to one that reflected the condition of the settlers. For settlers, the West was neither a romantic frontier, nor a naturalist's or ethnographer's paradise, but an empty and intimidating land out of which they had to make a home. A sense of homelessness is endemic to pioneer societies, and pioneer art naturally reflected the immigrant's need for reassurance as well as his hopes for the future. With settlement, art became internal, in both a geographical and a social sense.

Yet the change from documentary to reflective art did not happen overnight. Immigrants to the West in the last decades of the nineteenth century continued the propaganda of the CPR, the special artists, and the travel writers. Most were English or Ontarian and they too saw the settlement of the West as a thoroughly desirable extension of Anglo-Saxon society. Some may have had misgivings about the decision to leave home, but to have admitted them publicly would have been tantamount to a loss of faith. A popular and revealing form of communication was the illustrated letter. Designed to amuse as well as inform, the letters were invariably cheerful and jaunty and they conveyed an image of England transplanted onto the prairie. They admit to no serious loss of homely comforts and no radical changes of outlook and behavior. Taken together they support the view that the English came to Canada not to be "born free" as De Tocqueville put it, but to preserve the values and traditions of the old world.

Appropriately, the first resident painter in the West, following the departure of Peter Rindisbacher, was a dedicated imperialist.

Before he settled in Manitoba, Washington Frank Lynn had worked in London for the Canadian Land Immigration Company and he had been a founding member of the Royal Colonial Institute, a society devoted to the promotion of colonial affairs. Lynn's association with the institute led to visits to Ontario, in 1868, and to Kansas and Nebraska in 1871. In both places he reported on the fortunes of British emigrants and from his Ontario visit he returned a vigorous supporter of British emigration to Canada. He addressed meetings at the Colonial Institute and he wrote pamphlets under titles such as *Farming in Canada or Life in the Backwoods.* America he found much less accommodating. He was critical of the government for its neglect of emigrants on the journey west, for inequities in the system of land allocation, and for high rates of taxation. He was also disturbed by the prevalence of malaria.

Interested to see how the Canadian West compared to the American, Lynn traveled north from Nebraska to the new province of Manitoba in the summer of 1872. He found the Manitoba landscape—which he first saw from the deck of one of the Red River flatboats that supplied Fort Garry—to be a "flat and uninhabited waste," but when he reached the Red River settlement he was enchanted by the farmsteads along the river. Instead of the "miserable mud shanties or rickety boarded houses" of Kansas and Nebraska he found plastered log houses, white and neat, surrounded by haystacks, out-buildings, and patches of wheat. On the plain browsed small herds of cattle tended by "picturesquely garbed and dark-skinned little half-breed boys." Lynn was reassured by the demeanor of the Metis. While they looked and moved like Indians, they lacked the sternness and ferocity of the "wild and full-blooded warrior." Their "simple and good natured but

somewhat obtuse way," reminded him instead of honest gypsies and English agricultural laborers. Lynn was even sanguine about the Manitoba winter. He theorized that Lake Winnipeg and the valleys of the Saskatchewan and Assiniboine rivers were protected by their basin-like structure from the winter gales so common in Kansas and Nebraska. Yet, like Edward Roper, he was concerned not to be too flattering. Winnipeg jarred him. With the exception of Portage and Main, he found the streets to be in "the merest embryotic condition" and even on the two main streets, sidewalks and pavements were mere tokens: "a few broken bits of planking, with long and, in wet weather, muddy intervals between." Hotels were "rough," housing scarce, and rents "extraordinary." Emigrants were advised to make do with wagons and tents.

Lynn's intention had been to survey the Canadian West and to return to London and the Royal Colonial Institute, but he arrived in Manitoba too late in the season to make a thorough survey. Faced with the choice of wintering in Winnipeg or at one of the Hudson's Bay forts on the North Saskatchewan, he settled for Winnipeg where there was "more than enough to employ both pen and pencil." The delay was fateful. Save for a winter in St. Paul, Minnesota, which he liked even less than Winnipeg, he spent the next thirty years in Manitoba.

The only paintings by Lynn to survive are finished oils that date from his early years in Manitoba. Lynn had been admitted to the Royal Academy Schools in London but gave up a coveted studentship to cover the American Civil War as a correspondent for the Toronto *Globe.* At heart he was a reporter in the tradition of the specials and travel-writers. His Manitoba paintings are detailed and accurate and their general theme—the transformation of a land and a society by European

Frank De Forest Schook, *Alberta Homesteader—Pioneer Conditions*

Frank De Forest Schook, *Alberta Homesteader—After Four Years Effort*

settlement—was the stuff of reportage. To convey the theme he juxtaposed Indian and European ways of life. In one painting an age-old teepee stands beside a Red River flatboat and in another a European family picking nosegays is passed by an Indian couple returning with game from a day's hunting. Could two uses of the environment be more revealing? The paintings now seem elegiac but to Lynn they symbolized progress: a richly endowed land in the hands of a materially backward people was about to become a productive part of Empire.

Lynn's positive views of the West were sustained by painters like De Forest Schook who followed. Public optimism is *de rigueur* in pioneer societies. In the West at the turn of the century, it was reinforced by the success of the government settlement plan, a booming wheat market, and the general Edwardian confidence in human enterprise and material progress. Paintings, poems, and novels naturally reflected these buoyant sentiments. The preferred landscapes were those of the imagined future with nature "plotted and pierced" and otherwise transformed into settled land. Pioneers were cast in heroic moulds and the prairie was

converted into a land of golden promise. Poet Robert Stead caught the mood perfectly:

> For here on the edge of creation
> Lies, far as the vision can fling
> A Kingdom that's fit for a nation
> A Kingdom—and I am the king.

Bernard Smith labeled the similar phase in Australian society and art, "colonial heroic."

Western Canada's most effective exponent of colonial heroic sentiment was the restless English painter, Inglis Sheldon-Williams, who spent twelve years in the region between 1887 and 1917. Between his Canadian sojourns Sheldon-Williams lived in England or traveled—from 1899 to 1903—as a special correspondent for the English illustrated magazine the *Sphere.*

On arrival in Western Canada, Sheldon-Williams worked as a hired man on a farm at Brandon, Manitoba and then—he was not yet eighteen—filed for a homestead in his mother's name at Cannington Manor, a village in what is today southeast Saskatchewan. He was attracted to Cannington by the picturesque beauty of the country: "a park-like place of lakes abounding in all manner of wild fowl, rolling ridges crowned with poplar and willow groves and pleasant open spaces for building and cultivation." As the child of middleclass parents he was also attracted by the nature of Cannington society. The village had been founded in 1881 expressly to re-create in Canada the conditions of middleclass English life. The settlers built large, roomy houses which they appointed with furnishings, books, and pictures brought from England, and they engaged in such thoroughly English sports and pastimes as choral singing, amateur theatricals, cricket, tennis, and fox-hunting. Cannington was a short but "piquant chapter," as Sheldon-Williams put it, in the history of Western Canada.

Sheldon-Williams relished life at Cannington. "I lived," he wrote many years later, "in the atmosphere of Virgil's Georgics. . . . I rejoiced in the open life, the beauty of the great expanses under the always changing conditions, the storm clouds, the sunsets, the importunate stillness of night." Life in the settlement was also convivial. "We were young and full of life," wrote Lily Pierce, daughter of the founder of the settlement, "and had the great joy of being all together, and so we were very happy." In 1890 Sheldon-Williams drew for the *Daily Graphic* a

series of sketches showing how his solitary bachelor's life might be interrupted by the arrival on winter evenings of a group of festive neighbors. Pictures that dispelled well-grounded fears of the loneliness of pioneer life were then favored by the illustrated press.

Although pleasant and rewarding, life as a homesteader at Cannington didn't satisfy. Driven by an "urge to be a painter at all costs," he left for Paris and London in 1890. Sheldon-Williams was the son and grandson of painters. His grandfather had been a court painter to Queen Adelaide, consort of William IV, and his father, Alfred Sheldon-Williams, was a

Inglis Sheldon-Williams, *Ploughing the Fireguard,* 1903

recognized painter of animals and sporting subjects. Inglis came back to Canada in 1894 to complete the residential requirements that would give him title to his homestead and he spent the summer of 1895 on a ranch near Pincher Creek, Alberta. He returned to England in 1896, where he enrolled at the Slade School of Art, and in 1913 he came back to a booming Saskatchewan. His intention was to settle and establish himself as a painter in Regina. He received commissions for landscapes and portraits and in 1916 he accepted an invitation to begin a school of art at Regina College. But a life that consisted of "teaching a few girls to draw" while England and Canada

Inglis Sheldon-Williams, *The Fire Guardian,* 1903

Inglis Sheldon-Williams, *Threshing in Winter,* 1903

were at war was intolerable for a man of his temperament. He lasted only a year and 1917 found him back in England as an official Canadian war artist.

Although unable to settle in Western Canada, Sheldon-Williams was deeply affected by the life and the landscape and he wrote intermittently about both until he died. He regarded the West as a place where men were building "something that is going to count . . . [which] . . . grows and spreads from a shanty, a wood-pile and an axe." After 1913 he painted a number of genre or, as he called them, "subject pictures" of farming and rural life. The pictures have an epic quality; stalwart pioneers plough the virgin sod and pit themselves against an environment that assails them with biting cold, blizzards, and prairie fires. As celebrations of pioneer courage, labor, and rural life, they were probably influenced by the paintings of the Barbizon School of Northern France to which he was introduced when studying in Paris and London. The Slade School of Art in the 1890s was in the vanguard of contemporary art movements in England and, with the New English Art Club, founded in 1886 by artists with Barbizon and Impressionist sympathies, vigorously opposed the official art of the Royal Academy.

In London Sheldon-Williams was also exposed to the paintings of J. M. W. Turner and from them he learned how to suggest rather than define form and how, through the use of impressionistic techniques, to emphasize sky and light. Sheldon-Williams was one of the first painters to convey a sense of the stillness of the prairie, its emptiness and the luminous quality of its light. His prairie obviously was no Eden but neither was it, as it became in the work of later painters, a sleeping giant that in hostile mood could shrug off its human occupants. Rather than threatening settlement, Sheldon-Williams's blizzards, fires, storms, and cold simply gave it a dramatic setting.

Paintings that enlarged pioneer life filled the need for a sustaining myth that would carry the pioneers through the difficult, initial period of settlement. But bravado in societies as in individuals often conceals an underlying anxiety. The pioneers were not Davids bent on subduing a Goliath-like environment, but ordinary human beings faced with the problem of making a home out of a new and, as one of them put it, "naked land." Their dilemma was the subject of a poignant memoir by Welsh immigrant Evan Davies: "I felt very low and I believe David James did too. This was so unlike what we had imagined back in Wales. We had visualised a green country with hills around, and happy people as neighbours. No doubt a naive outlook . . . but one common to many people settling at the time. . . . There was something so impersonal about this prairie, something that shattered any hope of feeling attached to it or even building a home on it."

The instinctive response to an alien, intimidating landscape is to gravitate toward familiar features. Welshman David James chose a quarter-section with a ridge on it while the Ukrainians in Manitoba made for the

Inglis Sheldon-Williams, *Taking the grain to Market,* 1903

parkland because, as one of them remarked, "the woods and streams and meadows very much resembled our Carpathian scenery."

As well as choosing settings that reminded them of home, the settlers undertook physical changes designed to make the new landscape look more like the old. A landscape as intractable as the prairie allowed only token changes but whenever possible homesteaders built European-looking houses, planted trees, dammed streams to make ponds and lakes, laid lawns, and made flower gardens. They also named villages and towns after places in the homeland, raised European animals, and grew European crops. In cases of extreme longing for a familiar landscape, the transformation could take the form of an hallucination: "The sun would set on a perfectly white

plain, no dark object visible, everything covered with the white mantle of snow. After sunrise in the morning the plain seemed to be dotted with houses and trees, in one direction would appear a range of hills, in another a vast lake, and you would imagine you saw ships on it, then the scene would change and when you looked again you would see the same old familiar prairie."

So urgent a desire for a familiar-looking landscape was bound to affect the arts. When immigrant painters turned to the landscape they invariably converted it into prospects that would please European eyes. In most cases the conversion was probably inadvertent. In unfamiliar settings the imagination can follow one of two courses: it can find new means to express the new forms or it can make the new forms fit the old means. Pioneer painters usually followed the second course. In Western Canada, the temptation to impose external patterns was overwhelming; in many, perhaps most eyes, the prairie was a vacancy, not a landscape. Westward moving travelers in the flat, treeless stretches spoke of being "out of sight of land" while a stationary Jim Burden complained (in Willa Cather's *My Antonia*) that the prairie was "not a country at all, but the stuff out of which countries are made."

Schooled in conventional European approaches to landscape, pioneer painters had no formulae, or schemata, for such unfamiliar features as a clear, dry atmosphere, brilliant sunshine, sharp outlines, and, most perplexing of all, an almost featureless surface. Captain Butler, who had a painter's eye, saw the difficulties presented by a landscape bereft of the customary scenic props: "A view so vast that endless space seems for once to find embodiment, and at a single glance the eye is satiated with immensity. There is no mountain range to come up across the skyline, no river to lay its glistening folds on the middle distance, no dark forest to give shade to foreground or to bring perspective ... Reduced thus to its own nakedness, space stands forth with almost terrible grandeur."

Immigrant painters responded to the insubstantial landscape by isolating the few positive and familiar features—valleys, trees, hillsides, cattle, farmsteads—and treating them in known ways. "Like many other Canadians of the time," recollected one pioneer in Aileen Garland's history of the Killarney district, "my aunt saw little to interest her in the Manitoba landscape. She used pictures of English landscape as her models, changing and adding colour to suit her taste." Those particular paintings have not survived, but like the pioneer paintings in general they must have been European in character, sentiment, and style. Dark tones, restrained color, shadowy effects, soft outlines, and the suggestion of a pastoral mood combined to convert the prairie, as a modern critic has remarked, into a kind of Sussex.

In general the greatest distortions were suffered by familiar objects about which the painters had fixed ideas. Farmsteads were made to appear solid and substantial and trees were often given a full and leafy look. Occasionally, too, painters introduced pastoral features—sheep and wooden fences, for example—that were either missing from or uncharacteristic of the actual landscape. As in other parts of Canada the preferred subjects were always small, humble, and homely. The best-known examples in Canadian art are Cornelius Krieghoff's paintings of Quebec inns and houses. Aglow with warmth, jollity, and rustic charm, the paintings were everything that nineteenth-century Canada was not.

In prairie paintings, the most comforting features were farmsteads, valleys, and trails. In a landscape which offered "no place to hide," substantial-looking farmsteads that fitted snugly into the landscape and valleys that lay beneath the general surface, were symbolically identified with shelter. Wallace Stegner, who spent part of his boyhood on an exposed homestead on "bald" prairie in southwest Saskatchewan, explains the appeal of the valleys; "As the prairie taught me identity by exposing me, the river valley taught me about safety. . . . That sunken bottom (the Whitemud River) sheltered from total sky and untrammeled wind was my hibernating ground, my place of snugness, and in a country often blistered and crisp, green became the colour of safety. When I feel the need to return to the womb, this is the place to which my well-conditioned unconscious turns like an old horse heading for the barn."

Trails—a favorite motif—appealed because they represented space that, in Gaston Bachelard's phrase, invites us to come out of ourselves. Trails are beckoning features. They suggest a settled way of life, cooperative, purposeful behavior and, unlike the surveyed roads, sensitivity to topography. The old trails, as Hamlin Garland remarked, approached hills with caution and followed lakesides with leisure, and they did not rive, nor uproot, nor crush. To homesick emigrants craving comforting associations, a landscape without trails was unbearably foreign. Wrote one nameless Ukrainian pioneer:

> I found no path, no trail
> But only bush and water
> Wherever I looked I saw
> Not a native land—but foreign

Paintings that suggested correspondence between the old land and the new comforted the homesick and by preserving the patterns and traditions of the art of the old world they reassured settlers of the continuity of cultural ties. In pioneer societies art is an analgesic not a stimulant; realism appeals only to the comfortable and the secure. Anglicized versions of the landscape, which today seem either to evade the realities of the prairie or to distort them, satisfied such a pressing nostalgic need that the pioneers readily accepted them as true statements about the new land.

Two painters who adopted a reflective rather than an heroic approach to the land were James Henderson and Augustus Kenderdine. Henderson was a Scot who, before he emigrated in 1909, had attended the Glasgow School of Art and apprenticed as a lithographer and engraver. In Canada he worked as a lithographer and commercial artist, first in Winnipeg then in Regina. He disliked the flat, treeless Regina Plain and in 1915 he moved to the Qu'Appelle Valley, a glacial meltwater channel about a mile wide and two to three hundred feet deep on the northern edge of the plain. The valley claimed him so completely that, as writer Edward McCourt remarked, he forsook a larger reputation—that his talent might well have gained him—for peace of mind. Henderson lived in a cottage on the edge of Fort Qu'Appelle where he painted Indian portraits and landscapes.

Whereas the Regina Plain is flat and exposing, the Qu'Appelle Valley is a sunken oasis of lakes, molded slopes and beautiful wooded coulees set into the prairie surface. "There's no place in the world like our Valley," Henderson was fond of saying. He painted it at all seasons, usually early in the morning and in the evening, the quietest moments of the day. His paintings were benedictions in the nineteenth-century English manner and carried such evocative titles as *The Promise of Spring, Autumn in the Valley, Winter Glory, Qu'Appelle Valley,* and *Afternoon Sunshine*. They convey a sense of the delicate coloring of the prairie surface and the brilliant quality of the light but, confined to the valley, they do not so much as hint at the monumental nature of the land beyond.

Augustus Kenderdine was Henderson's contemporary. He was born within a year of Henderson, in 1870, and he came to Canada one year earlier, in 1908. Kenderdine was an accomplished and successful painter at the time of his arrival. His work had been exhibited at the Royal Academy and the Paris Salon, and some of it acquired by the Manchester Art Gallery, and the Grundy Gallery in Blackpool. Kenderdine had trained at the Manchester School of Art and, at the behest of his godfather, the Belgian painter Augustus LaFosse, at the Académie Julien in Paris.

Kenderdine first saw Western Canada from a CPR train window in 1904 while en route for Japan where he had family connections. He liked what he saw and, encouraged by friends who were Barr colonists, he returned in 1908 and filed for a homestead near Lashburn, Saskatchewan, in rolling parkland on a bench of the North Saskatchewan River. Nearby he found a lake and, in the words of his daughter, "the highest hill in the country." The hill so captivated him that he raised the house onto skids and hauled it with teams of horses and oxen to a point on the hillside where it overlooked the lake. "It didn't seem to matter," his daughter recollected, "that the hill—'Pike's Peak'—took up most of the one hundred and sixty acres, leaving a mere fringe to be cultivated. We all loved the place." As well as providing a view, the homestead contained a comforting piece of prairie history. The old Fort Pitt trail from Battleford to Fort Pitt, along which the Kenderdines loved to ride, lay along the edge of the lake.

Eight years later, in 1916, Kenderdine gave up farming in order to teach and paint. He was offered a studio and an instructorship at the university in Saskatoon, and in 1936, following the footsteps of Sheldon-Williams, he accepted an invitation to develop an Art Department at Regina College. Kenderdine remained in Regina until his death in 1947.

Like James Henderson, Kenderdine had no taste for the open prairie and when he did paint it he usually presented it romantically under such titles as *The Gathering Storm, Homeward Bound, Sutherland Trail,* and *Land of Promise.* His haunts were the valleys of the Qu'Appelle and the North and South Saskatchewan Rivers, and the woods and lakes of the north. His real refuge was the treeline. He loved, in his daughter's phrase, "the calm serenity" of the northern woods, and after the opening of Prince Albert National Park in 1927 he built a cottage at Emma Lake which became the nucleus for an influential summer school for the arts, begun by Kenderdine in 1936 and eventually taken over by the University of Saskatchewan.

Kenderdine found little to please him in the drought-stricken prairies of the late twenties and thirties, and one senses that, like the early travelers, he "traversed" quickly across them to find safe harbor in the woods and valleys. No realist, he painted only one picture of an abandoned, dried out farm. His disposition, as his daughter remarked, was to see only the beautiful in a landscape and where none was apparent he was, Charles Colgate intimated, inclined to invent: "He interprets the Western landscape more imaginatively than circumstances would require, and a preference for softly modulated tones and colours in his composition suggests that of the quiet solitude of the French paysage rather than the breeze-swept plains of the Canadian prairie."

A Native Vision: C.W. Jefferys and Prairie Landscape

Before a new land can be home it must, Northrop Frye has remarked, be confronted and imaginatively digested or absorbed. However unfamiliar and threatening, the elements of the new landscape must be translated into imaginative forms that correspond with the settler's experience of them. Images that merely mimicked the art of the old world may have comforted the homesick, but they were a palliative that in the long run only prolonged the sense of alienation. Art can be a mirror of the world but if it continually reflects other places, which purport to be the viewer's own, the result can be disquieting. People who are physically in one world, but dwelling spiritually in another, remain dissociated for as long as the world they inhabit is seen through the lens of another culture. The sense of dislocation affects not only the immigrants—but until the emergence of a national or regional vision—their children and their

children's children. Thus Margaret Atwood's laconic comment about Canada: "We are all immigrants to this place even if we were born here."

In the imaginative sense, the first immigrant painters made no attempt to engage the landscape, far less assimilate it to new artistic forms. Instead of confronting the prairie they merely transfigured it by selecting features that fitted old country formulae or by endowing the land and the pioneer with mythic qualities. Such transfigurations may have been a necessary support for insecure settlers but they could not sustain indefinitely. The challenge for painters who followed was to replace images of an unassimilated land, Frye's "predigested picturesque," with images consistent with the settler's experience.

The situation called for new eyes and new approaches. Painters unfamiliar with Canada and trained in Britain and France could not be expected to discard ingrained habits of perception and representation. Had he stayed in Canada Sheldon-Williams, with his feeling for prairie light and space, might have broken new trails instead of merely hinting at new directions. But, like the rest of the immigrant painters, he saw himself primarily as a bearer of culture to the new land, not as an interpreter of it.

A new vision could come only from within the country and from a painter determined to be led by his senses rather than by the precepts of academic studio painting. The first such adventurer, and deliverer of the West from a studio-bound vision, was Charles W. Jefferys of Toronto. Jefferys' credo was that art should aim for "the open sea and the high adventure." Adventure in art was the theme of an address to the Toronto Arts and Letters Club in 1911:

> There are today, as in the past, two main tendencies which, I think divide the domain of art, as they do the whole of existence. I may describe them roughly as a tendency towards order and the tendency towards disturbance. The one preserves, the other progresses; the one is necessary for harmony, for beauty, for complete expression; the other for vigour, strength, creative power—the thrill that makes art. To some—artists as well as laymen—art stands for a sort of sheltered garden, a sanctuary wherein to seek refuge from the work-a-day outside world, and forget for a time its crudeness and its cruelty. . . . In a new country like this, where life in general is crude, and regardless of little beyond material things, it is natural that the first conception of art should be that of the sheltered garden, where the finer spirits may dream awhile and forget the hurly burly.

Jefferys was born in England in 1869 but his family came to Philadelphia when he was eight years old and to Toronto, via Hamilton, when he was eleven. He apprenticed as a lithographer and in 1888 he joined the newly formed Toronto Art Students' League. The League, modeled after its New York antecedent, was a quietly nationalistic association of painters determined to find in visual art a style as authentic and as appropriate to the Canadian landscape as the style of poets Charles G. D. Roberts, Archibald Lampman, and Duncan Campbell Scott.

Inspiration came from two quarters: Scandinavia and France. An exhibition of Scandinavian paintings at the Chicago World's Fair, 1893—that later traveled to Buffalo and Toronto—provided members of the League with an opportunity to see the work of painters faced with a landscape similar to their own; one made up, as Jefferys put it, of "snow, pine trees, rocks, inland lakes, autumn colour, clean air, sharply defined forms." "We felt," he noted, "a natural affinity to them rather than to London, Paris, Munich and Dusseldorf Schools. We became northern-minded . . . [and] realised that on all Canadian painting . . . lay the blight of misty Holland, mellow England, the veiled sunlight of France." He insisted that Canada's affinities were with New England, Scandinavia, Finland, and Russia and not with "the foggy brown world wherein the sheep of Dutch pictures browse."

From France of the "veiled sunlight" came a second source of inspiration: impressionism. Canadians who had studied in France brought home the new method of open, or "plein air" painting in oil; "touches of primary colour," as Jefferys described it, "placed in juxtaposition which, viewed at the proper distance, gave a more brilliant representation of light and atmosphere. It was a seductive method that seemed peculiarly adapted to the high-keyed luminosity and the sharp clear air of mid-Canada." A style based on sensory experience not on academic precepts was just what Jefferys and the League had been looking for. Jefferys castigated the old methods: "Now with traditions and training such as these (i.e. French and English) how is the painter to deal adequately with an environment such as ours? Where can he find pigment which will fix upon canvas his response to the air and sunlight of a Western wheatfield? . . . He who approaches rural and pastoral Canada with the expectation of finding Europe in North America misses entirely its peculiar spirit."

To ensure the development of a distinctive Canadian style, Jefferys urged painters to travel throughout Canada, observing and experiencing its nature. He also encouraged them to sketch "à la Ruskin," a method that called for the close observation of the individual plants of field and forest. He was fond of saying that his real art school was the countryside. Jefferys practiced what he preached. He traveled indefatigably, visiting Western Canada alone several times between 1901 and 1924, and he subjected its landscape to minute scrutiny.

The occasion of his first visit was the Royal Tour—which he covered for the Toronto *Globe*—by the then Duke and Duchess of Cornwall, later His Majesty King George V and Queen Mary. Jefferys' attachment to the prairies was immediate and it was remarkable for occurring at a time when the eyes of visiting eastern and European painters were firmly set on the distant Rockies. Jefferys admired the mountains, but almost alone among painters, he felt no desire to paint them. He made a note of his first impressions of the prairie: "My first sight of the country which was to exert such an important influence on my career, was, when after crossing the more cultivated wheat belt of Manitoba,

the wonders of the prairies flashed upon my eyes in Saskatchewan and Alberta. . . . Words fail me to describe my impressions of that amazing land." Fellow reporters, who had just returned from the Boer War, compared the prairie to the Veldt, and Calgary to Pretoria.

In lamenting his loss of words Jefferys was, of course, unduly modest. His pen was as fertile and as talented as his brush and few artists have corroborated the evidence presented by their paintings with such articulate commentary. For Jefferys, the West represented one of the two basic topographic divisions of the country: "As to our topography we may divide Canada into two main types, one northern, the other western; one Laurentian, rugged, full of rocks, waterways, evergreen forest . . .; the other is a land of wide open spaces, of suave flowing lines, of harmonies of colour, of which the extreme type is the western prairie."

In notes and lectures Jefferys commented on the color, line, light, and texture of the prairie surface. The observations were so striking that they merit listing:

Pigments fail the ordinary colorist. Unable to rely on the conventional colour range, the "paint trekker" must fill his paint-box with many tubes of the brightest colours: pinks, blues, grass-greens and yellows soon run out, whilst purples and browns and all the deeper tones are rarely touched—this, of course applies to Fairy Prairie's summer dress."

Prairie like panther, tawny, indolent, fierce, lithe, feline, grace of line.

The interweaving graceful lines, the bending of the Bow. Illusive prairie reflects every mood of changing sky. A temperamental landscape.

Tough, wiry, furry, fuzzy prairie shrubs.

Long lines that tie the landscape together like ropes. All slight variations of horizontal, 45° rarity.

Here and there the claw shows through the velvet of feline prairie where jagged bare cut banks appear, gnawed and torn by rushing stream. Boulders and glacial drift, ancient beaches, seams and strata of rock and lignite emerge to reveal birth pangs of this softly rounded and gently moulded land.

Landscape that has no striking topographical shapes, that consists of earth, sky, light, air, reduced to their simplest elements and boldest features. In this severe austerity the grasses, the flowers, the shrubs, claim our attention, attract the eye and assert their individual charms. Vision becomes subtly discriminating, compares hues, tones, colours, all of them within a narrow range of what the artist calls values; yet under this compulsory and refined analysis, revealing an astonishing variety.

In spite of his enthusiasm for the prairies, Jefferys was not blind to the fact that his own sentiments were not general. Many of the immigrants were not, as he put it "fully acclimated" to the region. For the homesteaders the prairie was an extremely difficult environment as well as an unfamiliar one. It could unleash wind, hail, drought, and deep cold, and before it could be settled it had to be surveyed and fenced and the tough sod overturned; in a word, it had to be "tamed." The taming of the prairie, according to the ecologist Paul Shepard, was an expression of "nature hating": the imposition of an inflexible will, manifested by the unwaveringly straight lines of the rectangular survey, upon organic nature.

Among the European settlers of the prairie, only the ranchers stood outside the general context of struggle with the elements. Ranchers worked with rather than against the environment. Beef cattle occupied the ecological niche left by the buffalo and raising them was not usually toilsome. To survive ranchers did not have to "root, hog, or die." They lived not on the exposed flatlands but in coulees, where there was fresh water, wood, and even trout. At home in their surroundings, they planted fewer trees and made fewer lawns and gardens. The prairie was not always beneficent, but the ranchers were less vulnerable to wind, hail, and drought, and in the prairie grasses they had, thanks to sun-curing, a year-round supply of pasture and hay that in normal years was kept free of deep snow by chinooks. Success, other things being equal, depended on "knowing cow," ranching parlance for a sympathetic understanding of both the animal and the environment.

In the foothills of Alberta and the hill and coteau country of southwest Saskatchewan, the ranchers also had the most scenic landscape of the prairies. The combination of attractive, enfolding surroundings, freedom of movement, and a way of life manifestly in tune with nature appealed to residents and visitors alike. Lord Lorne declared in 1881 that if he had his life to live over he would be a rancher in Alberta, and in 1883 the editor of the Fort McLeod *Gazette* was forced to complain that he was "getting mobbed" by poetry that sang the praises of ranch life and the ranching country.

Enthusiasm for ranching and for the ranching country is also evident in painting. Ranching was presented less as an heroic struggle with environment than as an appealing and adventurous way of life. In Western Canada there were no cattle drives or cowtowns, nor, because of the presence of the North West Mounted Police, was there general lawlessness. But because ranching in Canada was a direct transfer from the States, it came with its romantic trappings of dress, speech, and names. The cowboys wore stetsons, spurs, and neckerchiefs, sat on tooled leather saddles, and worked ranches with such irresistible names as Turkey Track and Matador.

The ranching districts of Alberta and Saskatchewan produced only a handful of painters but two of the most notable, Roland Gissing and Robert D. Symons, were captive to the romance of the ranching life. Roland Gissing, nephew of the novelist George Gissing, was spell-bound by pictures of the West that he saw as a boy in Edinburgh. He emigrated in 1913 and for ten years he worked as a cowboy mostly in the American West and Southwest where he met the painter Charles Russell. He finally settled on a ranch at the junction of the Ghost and Bow Rivers just west of Calgary and was moved to paint by his intense feeling for the foothills and the ranching country: "I am inspired to paint firstly because I am so moved by the beauty of the Western scene. . . . I would call myself first and foremost a lover of nature and secondly an artist." In the twenties Gissing met C. W. Jefferys, who was a guest at a neighboring ranch, and was dissuaded from seeking instruction with the Art Students' League in New York on the grounds that the Bow River itself was a great natural art school. Gissing took the advice and became a popular painter of romantic foothill and mountain scenes.

Less conventional, artistically, was Robert Symons, son of the English painter and illustrator William Christian Symons. As a boy in Sussex he fell under the combined spell of Butler's *The Great Lone Land*—which he read and reread—and the *Farm and Ranch Review*, copies of which he obtained from a friend. His adventurous impulses may also have been stirred by Rudyard Kipling who was a visitor at his father's house. Symons emigrated in 1914 as a boy of sixteen and made for Maple Creek, then, as now, a main supply point for stock ranches in southwest Saskatchewan. Life as a cowboy met all his expectations. "What more could a youngster ask for than the sweep of a broken plain and the sunny sky, the fragrant prairie wind on his cheek, and a willing horse between his legs." Nor did the reality of the cowboy conflict with the myth: "But cowboys aren't spawned by accident. They are born that way. Men who love freedom, who stand up to a challenge, who love nature and wild animals and wind-swept places."

Symons also worked as a game warden and, until he discovered that he wasn't cut out for "dirt farming" he homesteaded in the rolling country west of Saskatoon. He tolerated ploughing because there was no outdoor activity that gave the naturalist more opportunity for observing certain birds. His strongest feelings were for the open rangeland of southwest Saskatchewan. "She is," he wrote, "a land you sometimes feel you hate; yet . . . you know she is a land you feel you cannot leave for long; she will call you back—back to the hiss of the ground blizzard, back to the starlit nights, back to the scent of willow and ground sage, back to the uplands of yellow grass where the horses gallop." For many years Symons was a correspondent for the Saskatchewan Museum of Natural History and painted almost entirely from memory the background murals for its habitat dioramas.

With Symons, as with Gissing, one senses that love of nature came first, painting second. Like Gissing he had no formal training as a painter but as a boy he was allowed to paint birds in a corner of his father's studio. When working as a rancher and game warden Symons made pencil and watercolor sketches of birds, animals, and incidents on the range. His work—much of it quickly done—was often crude, but as critics have remarked he understood how the landscape was formed and how things fitted together in it. He also mastered prairie light, atmosphere, and color; the ambers and grays of his early paintings gave way to lighter, clearer, colors—ochres, yellows, and greens that appear to be bathed in sunlight. He was, critic Terry Fenton concluded, a poet of place who was perhaps the purest observer in Saskatchewan art.

Regionalism and Realism: *The Art of L. L. FitzGerald, Illingworth Kerr, and Robert Hurley*

C W. Jefferys' exhortation to painters that they look afresh at the Canadian landscape, if heard at all in Western Canada, struck no responsive chord. The immigrant painters continued to paint as they had at home, substituting prairie scenery for English. Not until the twenties was there detectable change. Painters who arrived after World War I were less influenced by nineteenth-century approaches and, trained in the techniques of watercolor painting, they responded to the landscape with greater spontaneity. "Watercolor," as Walter J. Phillips remarked, "is the medium for impulse rather than meditation." By the twenties, therefore, prairie painting began to look slightly less like English art transplanted even though painters still tended to single out the more colorful and striking features of the landscape. Walter Phillips and A. G. Leighton were drawn westward to the mountains and foothills, while Alex Musgrove was attracted to the cluttered, dilapidated backyards of the old frame districts of Winnipeg.

A notable exception to the general run, both in terms of the subjects that he chose to paint and the ways in which he painted them, was Lionel LeMoine FitzGerald of Winnipeg. FitzGerald was born in Manitoba in 1890, and unlike the immigrant painters, his affection for the prairies never wavered. He spent the winter of 1921-22 studying at the Art Students' League in New York—where for the first time he saw paintings that were neither English or Scottish—and thereafter left Manitoba only for occasional visits to British Columbia. Night classes in Winnipeg with the Hungarian-born painter A. S. Kesthelyi, constituted his only other formal instruction. After retiring from the principalship of the Winnipeg College of Art, FitzGerald refused to be drawn down the retirement roads to the west and south. He liked the unambiguous nature of the Winnipeg climate, and its corollary—"freedom from uncertainty about whether it is winter or summer." Some of his finest paintings *(Doc Snyder's House* and *Pritchard's Fence)* were painted outside when temperatures were below zero (Fahrenheit). FitzGerald's only concession to the cold was to work in a small, stove-heated shack that he hauled about his yard on runners.

FitzGerald's childhood years were divided between winters in Winnipeg and summers on his grandparents' farm at Snowflake, south of Winnipeg near the US border. His country sojourns gave him, as he put it, "a solid feeling for the Manitoba landscape." Among his earliest recollections, he remarked in a radio broadcast, were "walks over prairie and dirt roads, and the sloughs with their fringes of willow, and the bluffs of poplar with their light trunks and shimmering leaves, the grass and the wild flowers that grew along the trails and always the sky." He was the first Western Canadian painter to see the landscape with a Jefferys-like acuity.

> I was more than ever impressed (on a journey from Winnipeg to Regina) with the wide variations in the contours from the flatness outside Winnipeg to the gradually increasing roll of the ground as we went westward. A marked blue in the distance gave the feeling of low lying hills and, sometimes, close up a higher mound, topped with trees, broke the long line of the horizon in a most pleasant way. Even where flatness dominated and the horizon seemed one long straight line, bluffs of poplar, farm buildings and the wide variety in the fields, from the light stubble to the dark of the freshly ploughed land, relieved the possible monotony and kept the interest.

FitzGerald's artistic range, like his geographi-

cal one, was also narrow. Except for an abstract phase toward the end of his career, he concentrated on landscape and still life. He painted sparely and carefully, apparently in the belief that by restricting his output and his geographical range he could intensify his vision. He went deep rather than far, as Robert Ayre so aptly put it. The inclination to go deep might have been connected with the taxing simplicity of the prairie. FitzGerald observed that a landscape in which conventional pictorial arrangements are few and far between defeated "mere picturemakers." He concluded that the country called for greater emphasis on patient observation than on picture-making.

Although FitzGerald was what John Constable would approvingly have called a "stay-at-home" painter, he was not a parochial one. As a young man he read and studied with the avidity of the self-taught. As a nationally known painter and principal of the Winnipeg College of Art, he also had a wide artistic acquaintance. He became a member of the Group of Seven in 1932, one year before the group disbanded. FitzGerald's artistic affinities with the Group were slight but he shared the Group's desire for a land-based Canadian art and the Group must have recognized in him the same questing spirit that united them.

Artistically, however, FitzGerald was a loner who adopted whatever approaches and techniques might help him resolve the problems presented by prairie space and light. His work has been linked with the impressionists, Millet and Cézanne ("my greatest influence"), but he espoused no school or master for very long. He began experimenting with impressionism early in his career and he used the impressionist's format of an expansive cloud-flecked sky and a sun-drenched, brightly colored landscape backed by a phalanx of distant trees. FitzGerald was absorbed with prairie sky and light and to give them full value he often used a vertical format with a very low horizon line.

FitzGerald found his true vision in his exquisite tree studies of the late twenties and the thirties. Throughout the twenties his drawing and painting became more precise as he sought ever clearer definitions of linear form. *Doc Snyder's House* and *From an Upstairs Window* are, in Dennis Reid's phrase, distillations of a life of looking and making. The paintings are now regional symbols, icons of the prairie winter that once seen, preempt forever our view of the stuccoed and poplar-studded landscape in the older parts of the towns. A treed yard in mid-winter will always be a capsule of stillness and of perfectly revealed form.

Illingworth Kerr and the Group of Seven

FitzGerald's preference for his ordinary, everyday surroundings was shared by growing numbers of Canadian and American painters in the twenties and thirties. The appeal of locality was associated with the slackening of European ties and the concomitant search for both regional and national identities. Painters, who were in the vanguard of the regionalist and nationalist movements, chose the land itself as the most appropriate symbol of identity. In each country the land had a commanding presence and it was widely believed that it had shaped the settlers. Novelist Frederick Philip Grove proclaimed in 1929 that national character was a product of the reaction of particular people to a particular place and that the reaction "tinged" attitudes to life and the world. Land and people were thought to be inseparable and it followed that by interpreting the land, painters would give people a stronger sense of who they were.

In America the land-oriented nationalist movement in art became known as the American Wave or the American Scene. Painters were encouraged to express the "spirit of the land" and, from a desire to throw off foreign influences, to "sing in their own voices or to stop singing altogether." The regionalist movement came to be associated with the agricultural heartland, the middle West, and with such middle Western painters as Thomas Hart Benton, John Steuart Curry, and Grant Wood. Paintings of commonplace scenes presented in ways that were easily understood became mirrors for Americans. Grant Wood's *American Gothic* is probably the best-known painting of the period. To celebrate the new nationalism the Whitney Museum of American Art, the first institution to house exclusively American painting, opened in 1931.

In Canada the nationalist standard, which had been raised by C. W. Jefferys and the Toronto Art Students' League was carried by the Toronto-based Group of Seven. In the introduction to the catalogue of the Group's first exhibition in 1920 Lawren Harris reasserted the need for a national vision: "An Art must grow and flower in the land before the country will be a real home for its people." To break the European hold on the Canadian imagination the Group chose, as representative of the country, a defiantly Canadian landscape—the Canadian Shield—and they painted it rebelliously: colors were bright and glowing, outlines hard, brush strokes vigorous and "chopped out," and forms isolated and abstracted. Artists in all parts of the country were encouraged to look at their surroundings through artistically unprejudiced eyes. In a cross-country tour arranged by the National Gallery in 1932, Arthur Lismer delivered about forty major addresses. He told his Regina audience that "art is not something imposed from without, and from another age, but . . . is something within an artist respond-

44

ing to the call of love and beauty. A love of one's environment is requisite."

The first Western Canadian painter to respond directly to the Group's proselytizing, and to the regionalist movement, was the Saskatchewan painter Illingworth Kerr. Kerr was born in Lumsden, in the Qu'Appelle Valley, in 1906. Encouraged by his mother, herself a watercolor painter, he began to sketch when still a boy. His first subjects were the mink, muskrat, and coyote that he trapped and hunted. His favorite boyhood pursuits were following game trails in the Qu'Appelle, and observing wildlife. Impelled by an urge to become an animal painter "and nothing else," he enrolled at the Ontario College of Art in Toronto in 1924. At the college, Kerr's interest in animals gained no encouragement; everyone, he recalls, was painting landscape. His teachers were Arthur Lismer, Frederick Varley, J. E. H. MacDonald, all members of the Group of Seven, and J. W. Beatty. In Toronto Kerr also renewed his acquaintance with C. W. Jefferys whom he had first met in Lumsden. Jefferys' base when painting in the valley was the Lumsden Hotel. Kerr recalls Jefferys saying, "wolf willow, lovely stuff to paint," a remark that made Kerr look more carefully at wolf willow and prairie vegetation in general.

In 1927 he returned to Saskatchewan "imbued by the nationalist spirit of the Group." He has written of his "bursting heart" at the first sight of the prairies on the journey home. Although his ambition was to see the prairie "with eyes unprejudiced by European influences," he quickly discovered that his training had left him singularly ill-equipped to realize it. In Toronto Kerr had learned to deal only with concrete forms and strong colors characteristic of the Group's own region, the Shield, and of most other parts of Canada—except the prairie. Visually, as Kerr has remarked, the prairie is an insubstantial land-scape whose bones are deeply buried.

With the exception of A. Y. Jackson the Group had no affinity, stylistic or temperamental, for the West. In Toronto Arthur Lismer had angered Kerr with his remark that the only interesting objects on the prairie were telephone poles. In the Alberta foothills, however, A. Y. Jackson found a landscape of smooth, rounded forms that was in some respects similar to the landscape of his favorite sketching grounds in the Laurentians. The bones and muscles of the prairie come to the surface in the foothills to form fluid sunlit hills and sinuous, shaded coulees. Jackson reveled in the rhythmic patterns and produced paintings and sketches that are charged with his sense of a vibrant, living landscape.

On his return to Lumsden, Kerr worked at a variety of seasonal jobs. Harvesting, sign-painting in the small towns, and trapping—in the Qu'Appelle and, for a season, in Northern Saskatchewan—took him outdoors and gave him time to paint. In the field he sketched whenever possible, braving sub-zero weather (when the paint was so stiff it could be applied only with a palette knife), blinding winter sunlight, lashing wind, dust and marauding mosquitoes and blackflies. Only on rare days is the prairie a suitable place for open air sketching. Kerr then was driven by what he has called a "passion" for nature, and the concentrated observation his mistress demanded, often in harmful conditions.

Through hunting and trapping Kerr developed an acute eye for landscape as well as for the animals hunted. He avows that there are few better ways of getting to know country than to hunt over it. True hunters develop what Carl Sauer called a morphologic eye, a capacity for the immediate recognition of significant form and pattern in the landscape. Kerr hasn't hunted or trapped since the Depression but he has drawn and painted animals throughout his career. His later drawings he now believes to have been acts of propitiation prompted by deep feelings of guilt for the animals killed. He suspects that all sensitive hunters and trappers suffer from a similar guilt complex. He points out the Indians would sometimes apologize to the animals they were going to kill.

Kerr converted his field sketches into finished paintings in a rickety studio above the pool hall in Lumsden where he "cooked in summer and froze in winter." Dust sifted through cracks in the walls and windows. Few paintings from his early period remain but among the survivals are scenes of Lumsden and the surrounding towns. They are the first realistic studies of the unkempt small prairie towns—"loose jointed," "gap toothed," and "sloppily put together" are some of Kerr's sharpest descriptions. He is severely critical of prairie design and architecture which he thinks is still mainly unrelated to the needs of the region. Straight streets that serve as wind tunnels, gables that catch the wind, and paint that peels in the hot summer sun are but a few of his targets.

Kerr's landscapes from this period are for the most part small, intense studies of the Qu'Appelle and the hill country of southwest Saskatchewan. Painted in strong, opaque colors and a powerful rhythmic style they were influenced by A. Y. Jackson's paintings of the Laurentians and Georgian Bay. Kerr has always felt a strong affinity for Jackson. He also admired the work of James Henderson, his artistic predecessor in the Qu'Appelle, but their views of the valley were antithetical. Henderson's valley is an enclosed world of gentle folds whereas Kerr's is a mere cleft in the massive prairie surface. In Kerr's paintings the eye is drawn inexorably to the hard, clear line that defines the shoulder of the valley and to the spaces lurking above it. To the inhabitants of Lumsden, Kerr recalls, the open prairie above the valley was "up on top."

When Kerr moved onto the plain his gaze never wavered. His paintings of the open prairie in winter were the first to register the stark qualities of its light and lines and to convey a sense of its awesome, inhuman scale. *Straw Stacks, March Thaw* (1935) is a milestone in the history of prairie landscape painting. Because it doesn't represent an actual place, it is also an example of an "idea" picture. "Idea" pictures were based on recollections of places seen when traveling or trapping or, more commonly, were scenes lodged in his unconscious that appeared as if by accident in his doodle drawings. Essentially they were distillations of his vision, imaginary scenes made up of features in the landscape seen over and over again. Kerr has also described them as archetypal or symbolic landscapes.

Although Kerr's paintings gained professional recognition through exhibitions in Regina, Saskatoon, and eastern Canada, very few of them sold. In Lumsden his only sales were to the proprietor of the Chinese cafe who bought several watercolors and three oils, which he gave to the Lumsden curling club. Thirty years later Kerr bought back the oils and removed the accumulated smoke and grime. One of the oils, *Last Light, Boggy Creek Valley,* is now in the collection of Saskatoon's Mendel Gallery.

Discouraged by the lack of sales and frustrated by a sense that his work was at a standstill, Kerr left the prairies in the mid-thirties. He was disturbed by his artistic isolation and found little relief from it in occasional contacts with the art community in Regina. He was, too, beginning to fear for his sight which had been damaged by exposure to dust storms and blinding winter sunlight. And, like thousands of prairie people, he wanted to escape from an environment sickened by drought and economic depression. In 1935, after burning most of his work, he shipped out on a cattle boat to England. In England, where his sight recovered in the mild air, he wrote and illustrated short stories for *Blackwood's Magazine.*

Kerr returned to the West in 1947, to teach at the Calgary College of Art, and he has painted the prairie landscape ever since. His favorite country is the foothills of southern Alberta whose gentle baroque and rococo folds, as he describes them, remind him of the Qu'Appelle Valley. Of all the painters to confront the prairie, Kerr has been the most articulate about the difficulties inherent in the subject. Although in thrall to its "very special mystique," he has no illusions about its artistic limitations. He regards the flat, open country as the "least inspiring environment for a painter." He elaborates: "For the visual artist the prairie is a great dome of sky, frequently cloudless, and often without much color, and a flat plain of earth receding to the horizon. If one sits on the ground to make a sketch, it all disappears behind the nearest weeds or grass." For the painter, the legendary spaciousness of the prairie is an illusion. Reduced to the dimensions of a canvas, the land appears as a narrow strip along the bottom of the painting. Kerr admits that he has never painted the prairie in a way that has truly satisfied him. Now in his seventies, he still speaks of the prairie as a "challenge," as an environment defying stock reaction and treatment that has still to meet its artistic match.

Robert Hurley

Illingworth Kerr was the first painter in Western Canada who did not, as Northrop Frye might put it, hide under the bedclothes when faced with the incubus of the flat, featureless prairie. Yet as a subject, Kerr found the prairie too limiting and since the thirties he has not painted it with any consistency. Mastery of the plain was the achievement of Englishman Robert Hurley. Diffident, slightly built, unlettered and untrained, Hurley was an unlikely giant killer. He was born in 1894 in Bromley-by-Bow, a picturesquely-named slum district of London. He came to Western Canada in 1923 and he dismissed the prairie, hyperbolically, as "a desolation—an abomination of desolation." He remarked subsequently that then he hadn't the eyes to see the prairie. Until the Depression he worked on farms and in lumber camps and to convey the flavor of his new life he, like many an immigrant before him, illustrated his letters home. He also began to sketch and he discovered that perspective came to him "as naturally as breathing." Until then his only expression of interest in painting had been occasional visits to the British Museum and the National Gallery in London where he was attracted particularly to the watercolors of John Sell Cotman. Hurley admired Cotman's "beautiful simplicity" and his capacity to eliminate inessentials.

Hurley's career in painting was launched by a chance meeting in Saskatoon in 1933 with the distinguished Austrian-born painter, Ernest Lindner, who was then teaching in the city. Although better known for his close studies of moss-covered trees and stumps in the northern forests, symbols of decay and regeneration, Lindner too has produced some more panoramic vistas of the landscape, capturing the prairie landforms, space, and light in such paintings as *Road and Fall, Thunderstorm* in the forties, and *Autumn in Saskatchewan.* Lindner's influence directly and through his association with the Emma Lake Artists' Workshop has been considerable.

Lindner encouraged Hurley to attend his sketching classes and informal weekly gatherings of painters at his home. Caught up in the general enthusiasm for landscape Hurley began, like his English predecessors, by painting the river valley near Saskatoon. Unemployed and unable to afford sketching paper he used the ends of rolls of newsprint; colors he extracted from beets, vegetable greens, and local clays.

Hurley's valley paintings were commonplace. His talent was for design and he could exercise it only when he moved away from the irregular terrain of the valley onto the settled, well-ordered plain. The straight lines of the horizon, roads, railway tracks, elevators and telephone poles, that jarred Romantic sensibilities, appealed to Hurley's sense of harmony and order. He acknowledged the geometric simplicities of the landscape and resolved the artistic problems they presented in practical ways. Hurley's instruments were a ruler, pen or pencil, and watercolors. He established space through the use of broad, watercolor washes, and the techniques of linear perspective. Watercolor is translucent and when applied in broad washes, it is an ideal medium for rendering prairie light and space. To master the effects of shadow and perspective, Hurley used cardboard models of elevators and houses and, later in his career, photographs taken from a low-flying plane.

Hurley's laboratory was the town of Sutherland, a railway divisional point of tracks, grain elevators, and telephone poles close to Saskatoon. His house looked onto an elevator and a railway track so that in winter he was able to paint without going outside. The front window of the house, as his biographer Jean Swanson has remarked, framed a typical "Hurley." Spring, when the sloughs were filled and Sutherland was awash with meltwater, was his favorite season for sketching. He was fascinated by reflections: "Did four pencil sketches of buildings reflect-

ed in pools of snow water. I love doing these." "Glorious day. Wandered around Sutherland. Six pencil sketches of elevators reflected in water pools." "Went scouting for pictorial ideas armed with sketchbook, pencils and water boots. Sky spectacular. Elevators reflected in water."

Hurley's paintings are distillations. He reduced an already spare landscape to its essentials: typically, to an empty foreground backed by silhouettes of elevators or a town and, to lend perspective, a railway track, a road, or a line of telegraph poles. The paintings are without figures, or movement of any kind. Their stillness, to borrow a phrase from Fredelle Bruser Maynard, is their reality. Scenes of winter and early spring are studies in austerity, the light harsh, the buildings stark and isolated, and the plain limitless.

Hurley described his prairie paintings as "potboilers," by which he meant paintings worked up from memory or from a pencil sketch. By changing perspective, composition, and minor details he could make several paintings from a single sketch. "I seem to have the happy faculty," he noted, "of recreating from the slightest thumbnail sketch, each time turning the trick into a fairly satisfactory Saskatchewan landscape." The elevators, tracks, and telephone poles that made up his paintings he referred to disparagingly as "usual stuff."

Although Hurley dismissed his potboilers, the paintings were, like many seemingly effortless productions, repositories of skill and fine observation. He had an artist's eye: "Within the confines of a few feet of fence run and snowdrift," he once noted,

I catalogued an extensive color range. A few scattered jackpine logs contribute browns, greys and purple, heightened with a rich orange band where a gleam of

48

sunlight touches. The pinkish tone of the snowbound stubble is emphasized by the greenish blue sky, and the tinned roof of a nearby shack has many variations of brown, grey, rust, black, sepia and purple, which would tax the palette of a master colourist. These treasures of the winter landscape are unobserved by the majority.

Hurley also has a remarkable capacity for suggesting, within a small compass, the spaciousness of the prairie. "Funny," he remarked when musing on the popularity of his pot-boilers, "how the public go for these telephone pole studies, plus a grain elevator or two, plus a vast sky with clouds, all within a 10 x 14 sheet. So much contained within so little." Critics too, marveled at his capacity for evoking space. Robert Ayre was astonished that the wide prairie horizon could be accommodated on so small a surface and he compared the economy of Hurley's means to the Chinese: "Hurley gives . . . us [the prairie] in its undramatic, almost featureless subtlety. In his sense of space, in his contemplative calm, in the delicacy and economy of his handling . . . he reminds me of the Chinese." The highest accolade came from Terry Fenton who regarded Hurley as "the first genuine painter of the prairies."

Hurley's compositions are now so familiar as to be visual clichés, but in the thirties and forties they were a revelation. His paintings sold as fast as his formularized procedures could produce them. Hurley kept no record of sales or gifts but he reckoned that he produced an average of five paintings a week for thirty years. The total, tabulated by Jean Swanson, came to 7800. The popularity of the paintings, which was immediate, was a classic example of the "shock of recognition." Tempered by pioneering and the hardships of the Depression, prairie people no longer needed the protection of the picturesque. It was as if, wrote Percy Wright in the Saskatoon *Star-Phoenix*, "they had been waiting for an interpreter who would point out to them the realities of their environment."

Contemporary Painting:
Abstract, Representational, Folk

Since World War II landscape painting in Western Canada has followed trails marked in particular by Robert Hurley and C. W. Jefferys. By selecting specific landscapes and painting them faithfully, Jefferys initiated a representational or topographical school of painting. Hurley's landscapes, on the other hand, were typical or symbolic. Hurley selected features characteristic of the general landscape and assembled them into pictures that emphasized the emptiness and the stillness of the prairie.

The two approaches correspond with the ways in which the prairie is seen. In a flat landscape the eye leaps from foreground to horizon—from, as Philip Fry put it, the grain of wheat to the big sky. Painters, then, must choose between the near or the distant, the parts or the whole. The choice, and the pattern it has imposed on prairie landscape painting, was noted by the reporter for the Saskatoon *Star-Phoenix* who reviewed an exhibition of

paintings by Robert Hurley and the English-trained Hilda Stewart in 1944. Both artists painted the prairie but they did so in entirely different ways. Hurley's paintings were notable for their clarity and simplicity; Stewart's for their delicacy and attention to detail. Hurley conveyed a sense of the awesome geometry of the land; Stewart of the subtle variations of its surface.

Hurley's gift to prairie landscape painting was to demonstrate the susceptibility of the landscape to abstract or symbolic treatment. His stereotyped town was an abstraction that acknowledged the difficulty of realizing the prairie artistically except by selecting a representative part of it, and presenting this as typical, or by constructing an assemblage of typical features. A landscape of simple, repeated forms invites abstract treatment. The outlines of the uncluttered surface, Sinclair Ross's heroine Mrs. Bentley remarked, "are so strong and pure in form they're just like a modernist's abstractions." She also declared that only a great artist could ever paint the prairie, "the vacancy and stillness of it, the bare essentials of a landscape, sky and earth."

Hurley's inspired simplifications were the first sustained abstracts of the prairie, but Hurley was not the West's first abstractionist. Both Illingworth Kerr and L. L. FitzGerald had abstract phases. Kerr's first abstracts were his "idea" pictures that appeared accidentally as images—summoned from his unconscious—in his doodle drawings. As expressions of conceptual rather than perceptual truth, they squared with his conviction that the prairie painter must settle for an equation for nature: "I was painfully aware that realism the [literal aspect of nature] must throttle the prairie artist. Space seemed incompatible with the means at my disposal." He became convinced that the answer to western space, with its "vast scale and power of mood rather than tangible form" lay in abstraction, and in 1954 he sought out Hans Hoffman, the German abstract expressionist. Kerr found the association with Hoffman rewarding but admits that he has never applied Hoffman's methods successfully to the prairies.

FitzGerald's abstracts were also a product of the fifties. Determined to reduce an already spare landscape, he developed a "sort of shorthand" that allowed him to get down "the essentials . . . in the fewest possible lines." FitzGerald's abstracts, like Hurley's and Kerr's, were distillations based on "stored up" memories. "Occasionally," he wrote, "I get out onto the prairie just to wander and look without making any notes other than mental ones . . . I seem to require this freedom, for the present, from the thing seen and its restrictions." He discovered that the landscape entered the far corners of his psyche: "the prairie and its skies," he noted, "get into most of the things I do."

Landscape also pervades the work of more recent abstractionists. Neither Takao Tanabe nor Otto Rogers, to take two of the most eminent, considers himself to be primarily a landscape painter but it is unlikely that either would paint as he does had he not lived on the prairies. Both painters were strongly affected by abstractionist tendencies in art during the fifties and sixties and saw in the large paintings of Rothko and Hoffman, with their bands of pure color, a means of tackling the vast prairie landscape. Each has adopted large canvases, broad areas of flat color, and simple divisions of space to produce images that are sometimes compelling.

Their work, like that of all abstractionists,

L. L. FitzGerald, *Landscape* (Abstract), 1950

is symbolic rather than specific. They describe qualities of light and space and the general relationships between land and sky, not particular places at particular times. Tanabe's forms in particular have become progressively simpler and softer, resolving finally into a series of undulating color relationships. His paintings are without hills, trees, or rivers, and perhaps to distinguish them from conventional landscapes all are entitled *The Land.*

Otto Rogers is equally careless of conventional form. His landscapes too, are distillations: "I've never gone out into the landscape and worked directly from it. I find it too confusing because I get caught up in the details. But if I spend an afternoon in the country and then I come home and paint, I think that whatever I took in . . . tends to get concentrated in the painting."

Philosophically Rogers, who is a Baha'i, does not distinguish between the solid and the ethereal, matter and spirit. As a youth in Kerrobert, Saskatchewan, his eye was drawn to the line of the horizon where, in his phrase, "earth meets sky and matter nothingness." The apparent melding of land and sky that occurs on the prairie at certain seasons and under particular atmospheric conditions has become, in his paintings, a metaphor for his vision of reality.

Rogers' first impulse toward art came on his journeys to school and on his walks around the family farm. "The view in every direction was endless. I was suspended in time and space and took constant delight in the diversity of color and form. I was happy. I danced with my spirit and floated everywhere in the air like a figure in a Marc Chagall painting." Rogers, as critic Robert Enright remarked, is a light meter who absorbs and measures prairie expanses and reflects them back to us in his paintings. Few painters have expressed so well the luminous, enveloping quality of prairie light and the expanding nature of its space.

Two abstractionists who address the prairie directly are Norman Yates and Robert Sinclair, both of Edmonton. In his "land studio," a quarter section of fields and poplar bluffs in the parkland west of Edmonton, Yates paints "landspace," a neologism coined to suggest the unbounded nature of prairie space. The connotation of landscape, argues Yates, is of a prospect that can be taken in at a single view. Yates expresses prairie landspace through large canvases divided into strips of land and sky. The light is hard and colors are correspondingly sharp and vivid. Unlike most abstract or non-representational works, Yates landspaces are peopled. The figures—small, faceless and semi-transparent—seem absorbed by the light and space. They are meant, says Yates, to express a synthesis of man and nature. He regards land as the basic prairie metaphor and contends that prairie history is "integral with love for the land." Discard that love, he warns, and "we lose our own soul."

Unlike Yates, Robert Sinclair seems untroubled by questions of love and hate for the land. Sinclair's regional emblem is the prairie road. Symbolizing movement, promise, and hope, roads are universally acceptable symbols but on the prairies they have a particular appeal. They offer release from the tyrannical distances and protection from prairie space. To be unwheeled and immobilized on the exposing prairie flats is to be defenseless. So essential is the automobile to prairie life that the characteristic view of the landscape is through a car window. Reduced to a road, its shoulder and a patch of sky, Sinclair's prairie is the ultimate distillation.

Representational Painting

Abstraction may be the most recent tendency in prairie art, yet most painters continue to paint the landscape in conventional ways. Landscape painting in its traditional forms flourishes in the West as in no other region of Canada. Bruce Ferguson, a Montreal juror at the 1982 Saskatchewan Open Exhibition of the Arts, was overcome by its predominance. Ferguson's version of "landskips! Landskips!" was "Grain elevators, sunsets, barns, trees, tractors, snowdrifts . . . all rendered in the traditional media of paint and graphics." Even the occasional abstract, he noted, was rooted as much in the landscape tradition as in modernist theories.

Ferguson concluded that such single-minded concentration upon landscape must be the expression of a collective sensibility that is thoroughly bound to the land and rural life. The prairie population is now predominantly urban but most people are barely a generation removed from the land. Scratch a Westerner and you will find not a Tartar but a farmer. Paintings of landscape and rural life affirm the Western identity or they touch, to borrow a phrase from Norman Yates, the West's psychological core.

Another strong reason for the popularity of landscape painting is the compelling presence of the land itself. The prairie is never just background. Nature dominates even in the cities. Blizzards and dust storms roar in across the unprotected and unprotecting plain; low, thinly spread buildings do little to mask the overarching sky; and broad, straight streets lead the eye outward to the country. The prairie demands attention, and because it lies outside the scenic lexicon it also demands definition. Mountains and the sea are now such visual clichés that it takes an effort of will to see them except as pictures. But a scenic Cinderella, for which there are few templates to preempt perception, can be seen with fresh eyes at each approach. For painters the prairie is a perpetual challenge.

Painters who approach the landscape conventionally aren't easily categorized but most can be placed in one of two rough groups. For the majority of painters the landscape is an end in itself and they find interest and beauty in its rivers, farms, fields, and villages. Others, however, see the landscape primarily as a setting for human activity and in their paintings they comment on prairie history and society.

Two distinguished members of the first group are Reta Cowley and Dorothy Knowles. Early in their careers they were attracted to abstract approaches presented by painters of international standing who conducted workshops at the University of Saskatchewan's Emma Lake Summer School. But in neither case did abstraction take. Each quickly turned to conventional or representational treatments of landscape, achieving quality and originality by painting close to nature. For example, Reta Cowley always paints out of doors. Painting from sketches or slides she regards as more of an exercise than an adventure. Prairie wind and weather are stimulants, as is the problem of fixing a particular moment in time: "Nature is constantly changing. I look up and see a color and I record it. The next time I look up the color is no longer there, but I see another color somewhere else. Gradually my painting is built up of these patches of color."

The method obviously is designed for small, comprehensible landscapes, not broad sweeps of nature. When she finds a setting that she particularly likes she goes back to it again and again, subjecting it to Jefferys-like scrutiny. She is drawn, for example, to farmsteads in low hollows that are almost engulfed by the landscape. If the location hasn't a name it is usually given one and its position is described on the back of the picture. No approach could be less generalized or abstracted. Reta Cowley paints particular places at particular times, capturing in watercolors and acrylics the delicate, shimmering qualities of prairie trees and shrubs and their subtle colors—from the fresh greens of spring to the mellow oranges and yellows of the fall.

Dorothy Knowles also paints out of doors, but unlike Reta Cowley and most contemporary landscape painters, she works on large canvases on which she conveys an illusion of bulk and depth. Critics have compared her vistas to the vistas of classical landscape painting. Knowles grew up on a farm situated on the rim of a long, deep valley near Unity, Saskatchewan. The valley, as she describes it, was five or six miles across and all hills and gulleys. Valleys and rolling landscapes are now her stock-in-trade. She returns to them again and again, laying in the outlines of the land in charcoal before applying her characteristic colors—buffs, browns, and greens—in acrylics and thin oils. Like all successful painters of the prairie she is able to create effects of intense light. She has also been instrumental in dispelling the illusion that the prairie is an unrelieved plain. Her paintings evoke not only the scale of the prairie but also, as Toronto's Bernie Hale has remarked, its "rolling, teeming, folding, incredibly rich bulk."

Reta Cowley and Dorothy Knowles are merely preeminent members of a large body of accomplished landscape painters now at work in Western Canada. Two less well-known but venerated painters are Ruth Pawson and Dorothy Martin. Both studied at Regina College in the late thirties with A. F. Kenderdine from whom they learned a lesson that was particularly salutary for painters of the prairie. Kenderdine sent them into the country to sketch and when they returned empty-handed with the excuse that they could find nothing to paint, Kenderdine retorted that there was always something to paint. "Until

that moment," said Dorothy Martin, "I used to think it was the duty of nature to find us subjects. Now I realize that it's our duty to find something in nature."

Ruth Pawson, whose training was the more extensive, also studied with A. Y. Jackson. From Jackson she learned how to paint indefatigably and only those subjects about which she was enthusiastic. Jackson taught her to identify the molded forms of the land and the rhythms in the wind-swept grainfields. The wind, says Pawson, forces the landscape into life.

Motivated only by love of the landscape and a desire to paint it, both women have spent a lifetime prowling prairie backroads in search of subjects. Throughout the fifties and sixties when prairie, and Regina art in particular, was in thrall to the abstract New York school, they suffered neglect, even contempt. The disinterested spirit in which they worked was summed up by Dorothy Martin in a remark of touching artlessness: "When you've finished a picture and you sign your name, I always would like to put 'with love from Dorothy.' Because that's what I feel."

Today, love of the prairie is by no means confined to the native-born. One of the region's most ardent admirers is Joe Acs, a Hungarian who lives in Edmonton. An escapee from the 1956 Revolution, Acs was captivated—after the turmoil of Hungary—by the quietness of the Alberta parkland. He also liked its clean and uncluttered look. To outsiders the prairie may seem flat and monotonous but for Acs it has "a grandeur that cannot be described in words." He feels "very poetic" about the prairies and has done so ever since reading about them as a boy of sixteen. His serene vision of the landscape is reflected in paintings that show tranquil villages, golden wheatfields, and untroubled skies. Acs' artistic interests extend beyond the highly detailed Alberta landscapes for which he is best known. Especially important is the expression of emotion or involvement with the scene depicted, a quality evident in both his on-the-spot and studio paintings.

Paintings that present the prairie as a stable, well-settled land may be true for given moments but from a social and historical point of view they can be misleading. In spite of its productivity, and the permanence of its fields and roads, in a sociological sense the prairie is in upheaval. Settled less than a century ago by a flood tide of immigrants, the rural districts have been emptied of people. The tidal ebb, that carried the bulk of the farm population off to the cities, left a flotsam of abandoned farm buildings, rusting machinery and rotting fence lines. These are now as much icons of the prairie as the sturdy grain elevators.

Painters who choose to comment on prairie history and society concentrate on this landscape of dereliction and decay, not on the living landscape of productive farms and fields. Examples are R. G. Pollock of Winnipeg and, most notably, George Jenkins, now of Victoria. A socialist, Jenkins believes that a painter should make social and political statements: "A plough in a field can be a landscape but the abandoned field in the background gives the painting social significance and the work takes on an entirely different meaning."

Jenkins grew up near Wilkie, Saskatchewan, on a farm whose roads and fields are "etched" on his mind. He began painting when working in logging camps on Vancouver Island just after World War II but it wasn't until 1969, at the age of forty-nine, that he decided to become a full-time painter. He was on a visit to the prairies: "The landscape hit me in a powerful way, absorbed me. Then I got into painting for my life work." He sold his first four paintings to the Mendel Gallery in

Saskatoon and subsequently he has scarcely been able to keep up with the demand for his work. He rarely has enough paintings on hand for an exhibition.

Although he rejects the label self-taught, Jenkins has had no extensive formal training; he learned to paint by reading, looking, and doing. He perfected his method of painting—"abstract realism"—long before he knew it had a name. The method calls for the elimination of inessential details and for the utmost care in painting what remains. Objects appear with an unnatural, dream-like clarity that gives the paintings an eerie, abstracted look. Buildings that formerly were alive now house only memories and a landscape that once was peopled is occupied only by ghosts—lonely, isolated figures summoned from the painter's past. "I suppose," says George Jenkins, "I represent society as being anti-social."

The disappearance of the pioneer landscape, and the communal way of life it is thought to have contained, has occasioned widespread feelings of regret. The landscape of small farms and closely spaced towns and villages, that both planners and pioneers had envisaged, lasted for only a few decades. Farm enlargement, mechanization, and the lure of the cities emptied the countryside as quickly as the settlement plan had filled it up. There isn't, to quote a current refrain, anybody out there. Gone, too, is the textured landscape of bluffs, barns, fences, and hayfields to be replaced by large unbroken fields and standardized farmsteads—the mechanistic landscape of agribusiness.

In spite of strong European associations, nostalgia is not an exclusively European sentiment. It is the prevailing sentiment in the paintings of Allen Sapp, a Cree Indian from the Red Pheasant Reserve near North Battleford, Saskatchewan. Encouraged by Allan Gonor, a local physician, and tutored by

Wynona Mulcaster, a noted landscape painter and a professor of art at the University of Saskatchewan, Sapp has become an accomplished and popular painter. Although Mulcaster knew no Cree, and Sapp little English, she was able to teach him valuable lessons about structure, form, and color. Sapp's colors are cool and northern—whites, blues, and grays accented by flecks of bright color. His subject is reserve life during the thirties and forties which, like prairie life in general, seemed sweeter than it is today. Indian life during Sapp's childhood was in some respects not noticeably different from the life of poorer European settlers in the parkland. Both groups, at slightly different times, lived in mud-chinked log cabins, and cut wood and hauled water in much the same ways. Buyers of Sapp's paintings, it goes without saying, are middle-class whites who see their own lives, or the lives of their parents, mirrored in his work.

Folk Painting

Nostalgia for the past, coupled with a genuine pride in pioneering and a desire to record the experience, is clearly reflected in the folk art of the region. Most folk artists take to painting relatively late in life, usually from a desire to record the past. "Instead of writing my memoirs," remarked former schoolteacher Eva Dennis, "I am painting them." Her husband Wesley Dennis was equally direct: "I take pleasure in painting the farm scene as I knew it from pioneer days to modern times."

Folk art is the most regional of all art; folk artists paint directly from experience so their paintings are always anchored in time and place. Incidents and events are recalled in memory and set down artlessly on board of canvas. Things far may be brought near, perspective ignored, and space treated in a two-dimensional fashion. The paintings rec-ord a mood, a spirit, and the painter's feelings about his, or her, life and place. They tell us not so much what the past looked like but what it felt like to be in it, at least some of the time.

Although true for particular moments in the past, folk paintings do not represent the whole of pioneer life. Memory is notoriously selective, and it simplifies and composes our perceptions. Jan Wyers' *These Good Old Thrashing Days* is a delightful painting that expresses the energy and exuberance of the early settlement, but threshing as any old-timer will tell you, was one of the least pleasant jobs on the farm. The noise was deafening and the dust choking. Isolation, loneliness, discomfort, and economic insecurity—the very conditions that caused the exodus from the farms—do not figure in the folk record. Yet in spite of a tendency to idealize the past, and of crudities in execution, folk paintings have an authenticity that is sometimes missing in gallery art. They are untouched by schools and fashions, and the feelings that inspired them, however selective, came always from the heart.

Paintings that evoke the past kindle memories of childhood and youth when life seemed simple, pleasant, and secure. But although dreams of a lost Eden are alluring, nostalgia alone cannot explain the profound feelings for place that such paintings sometimes evoke. Adult memories of childhood, even when they are nostalgic, seldom suggest the need to be a child again. More often, they refer to the more limited desire to see the world in a child-like way, to feel at one with the environment, to be at home on earth. The regional world is the world of childhood and home, and Western Canadians have been blessed with two peerless exponents of it: the writer W. O. Mitchell, and the master painter William Kurelek.

Kurelek was a supreme individualist. In his relatively short life—he died in 1977 at the age of fifty—he followed his vision with a sublime disregard for fashion. He took a degree at the University of Manitoba and then attended art schools in Mexico and Toronto. But neither school satisfied and he decided that he could learn to paint only by doing. To all intents and purposes he was self-taught. He settled in Toronto where he worked as a picture framer at the gallery of his first sponsor and exhibitor, Avrom Isaacs. He painted in all parts of Canada as well as in England, Russia, and India but his true center lay in the Ukrainian districts of Manitoba. He painted best in places that were open to the sky and he felt most comfortable, figuratively speaking, with men in sheepskin coats—the common folk of whichever country or region he happened to be in. Kurelek's lumpy, anonymous figures stand for all men, and their triumphs and trials are common to mankind.

Four themes, as the historian Ramsay Cook pointed out in a loving and perceptive essay, dominated his work: childhood, the prairies, Christianity, and the Ukrainian settlement. Kurelek observed wryly that he was seen either as a portrayer of farm life or as a missionary in paint. He was unabashedly Christian. He espoused Roman Catholicism after a profoundly troubled youth and early manhood and for the rest of his life was an affirmed proselyte. Paintings that had no specifically religious or prophetic content he dismissed, shades of Robert Hurley, as pot-boilers. But so insistent was the demand for vernacular, and especially prairie, works that he was forced to meet it even though he was often frustrated by having to do so. He was preoccupied with what he felt to be the precariousness of man's existence on earth and felt bound to warn of the folly of aggression, greed, and materialism. Like Brue-gel, to whom he is often compared, he could not resist allegory.

The themes of childhood and the prairies are as inseparable in Kurelek's work as they are in W. O. Mitchell's. *A Prairie Boy's Winter* and *A Prairie Boy's Summer* are visual analogues of Mitchell's *Who Has Seen the Wind?* Kurelek's imagination, like Mitchell's, fed on memories of childhood and, like all gifted artists, he retained the capacity to see the world with a child's unmediated vision. He didn't, as Wallace Stegner remarked, separate what he saw from what he knew and so make perception serve inference. Thus the startling clarity of Kurelek's paintings and the completeness of the world they represent. In psychological terms they are good gestalts, perfect microcosms that manage, through the presentation of simple, everyday events, to convey entire worlds.

Kurelek's imaginative home was his parents' house near Stonewall, Manitoba, about nine miles north of Winnipeg. The house appears in many of his paintings. Kurelek felt a particular attachment to the bogland east of the family farm and when he returned there in 1963 he wrote to Avrom Isaacs in Toronto: "The vastness of the prairies with occasional clumps of poplar bushes gives me a feeling of communion. No one seems to understand why I am so fascinated by this place, not even the local people. Only I it seems can express it though others may feel it inarticulately." Here, as Ramsay Cook put it, "was home, what the Spanish call *querencia*, contentment of familiar surroundings. A sense of identity."

Around Stonewall lay the settled parkland of Manitoba whose fields, farms, and roads, and the people who made them, were Kurelek's staple subjects. The landscape he regarded as a vast stage for a human drama that he found both heroic and frivolous. His vantage point was always elevated and by keeping his horizon line high he was able to convey a sense of the table-like immensity of the land. Kurelek's prairie is a solid platform and in spite of his views of the precariousness of man's tenure on earth, his figures have the perennial, indomitable qualities of Bruegel's peasants.

Kurelek was also a masterly painter of skies which were often, to use John Constable's phrase, the keynote of his pictures. In the flat landscape they were the chief source of drama and in allegorical paintings they could be used to heighten effects. What better vehicle for an apocalyptic vision than a prairie thunderstorm, or, for a vision of the sweetness of the earth, the candy floss cumulus of a summer sky.

But Kurelek was a painter before he was an allegorist. He couldn't resist the appeal of prairie skies and no one has painted them more effectively. Seasonal changes in cloud formation and in the color of the sky were recorded with great accuracy. He acknowledged his obsessive interest in skies. "I photographed the skies all afternoon and when night fell I worked on my paintings by the light of the car ceiling. I still get a shudder of awe sometimes when I look at that series of photos in my album." And of another afternoon's skying he wrote: "But I love doing skies. . . . Almost miraculously the sky took over. I worked fast, loosely, intensely with a big brush, a colour soaked rag and a dry rag. I could hardly believe my eyes how it turned out." As if astonished by his good fortune he exclaimed humbly, "This is real creativity God's blessed me with."

Kurelek's fourth theme was the life and labors of Ukrainian people in Western Canada. In painting after painting Kurelek demonstrated that Ukrainians, who were often dismissed by the dominant Anglo-Saxons as slow-witted Slavs, "Galicians," were not only capable and hard-working but that they had a rich and colorful culture. His most deliberate statements were made in unified series of paintings: *An Immigrant Farm in Western Canada* (1964), *Ukrainian Women Pioneers in Canada* (1967), and *A Ukrainian Pioneer* (1980). The series, together with many individual paintings of the migration and settlement, are a comprehensive record of Ukrainian life in Western Canada. When honored for his accomplishment by Alberta Ukrainians Kurelek was characteristically "overwhelmed" by the esteem in which they held him.

An essay on the history of landscape painting in Western Canada culminates naturally in Kurelek. Like all great regional painters, he embraced a place and a people and he made them peculiarly his own. Painters will continue to paint the prairie but it is unlikely that any will challenge his claim to the farmed and settled landscape. Kurelek had the gift, rarely given, for what Ruskin called seeing to the heart, and it gave his paintings authenticity. They seem certain to govern perceptions of the twentieth-century prairie landscape in the same way as the paintings of L. S. Lowry govern perceptions of industrial England.

EPILOGUE

For Ukrainians, as for all immigrants, the journey to the new land was a spiritual odyssey as well as a physical one. Migrants to the West crossed an ocean or a continent to find a land stranger than most of them could even have imagined. Adjusting to it psychologically was as difficult as adjusting physically. Landscape painting on the prairies is a record of that adjustment, even when allowance is made for discrepancies between what the artists saw and felt, and, constrained by the demands of style and taste, what they painted. Appreciation of the spare, austere qualities of the prairie required the development of a new sensibility, and an aesthetic based on scarcity not romantic or picturesque fullness. Support for the assertion can be found in the architecture as well as in the art of the prairies. Eclecticism still rules prairie architecture, but in recent times appreciation has grown for the simple, streamlined forms of the curling rinks, potash plants, and farm machinery sheds.

But the transition from romanticism to realism in prairie art was more than an exercise in perception and aesthetics. As well as being a new venture in art, the development of a native vision expressed a profound spiritual need. In an essay recalling his youth in Manitoba, W. L. Morton, the distinguished historian, wrote of the impossibility of reconciling the actual and the mind's landscape in a region whose arts lacked a native vision. The landscape Morton lived and worked in was Manitoba prairie but the landscape in his mind's eye, formed by reading English books and looking at English pictures, was European. He experienced the tension of a mind that was not connected imaginatively to its surroundings. In retrospect, he concluded that "no country can be really owned except under familiar name or satisfying phrase. To be apprehended by the mind and made personal, it requires not only the worn comfort of a used tool or a broken-in shoe; it requires also assimilation to the mind, ear, eye and tongue by accepted, or acceptable description in word, or line, or color." At bottom, Morton's observation is ecological; a sense of place is a human imperative and without it there can be no integration of the self with the environment. Prairie landscape painting may therefore be regarded as a record of man's halting, spiritual adaptation to a singular and difficult environment.

Art Before the Settlement

Charles Adolphus Murray (Seventh Earl of Dunmore), *Souris River*, ca. 1858–62

George Seton, *Indian Dog Feast,* 1857

R. B. Nevitt, *On the March West,* ca. 1874

R. B. Nevitt, *Fort Calgary in Summer,* ca. 1876

William Armstrong, *Post Dog Trains Leaving Fort Garry,* 1851

Peter Rindisbacher, *The Governor of Red River*

Peter Rindisbacher, *Winter Fishing,* 1821

Peter Rindisbacher, *A Souteaux Indian*

W. G. R. Hind, *Settler's House and Red River Cart*

W. G. R. Hind, *Duck Hunting on the Prairies,* 1862

W. G. R. Hind, *Camping on the Plains*

W. G. R. Hind, *A Prairie Road*

Paul Kane, *The Man that Always Rides,* ca. 1850

Edmonton House

Paul Kane
1846

Paul Kane, *Fort Edmonton,* 1846

Paul Kane, *Fort Edmonton,* ca. 1850

Frederick Verner, *Indians by Hut and Canoe,* 1900

Frederick Verner, *Buffalo Grazing,* 1889

Henri Julien, *NWMP Killing Ducks,* 1875

Henri Julien, *The Sweet Grass Hills, 1875*

Within the image: *unfinished*

Some Prairie Flowers and a Prairie Dog

Broadview Assiniboia, N.W.T. Canada Aug. 4, 1887

Edward Roper, *Prairie Flowers, 1887*

Edward Roper, *Breaking the Prairie*

Edward Roper, *A Settler's Home*

The Art of the Settlement

Washington Frank Lynn, *The Forks*

Washington Frank Lynn, *The Dakota Boat*

Inglis Sheldon-Williams, *After the Storm,* 1914

Inglis Sheldon-Williams, *The Landmark,* 1916

Inglis Sheldon-Williams, *The Fireguard,* 1923

James Henderson, *Winter Glory, Qu'Appelle Valley,* prior to 1936

James Henderson, *Afternoon Sunshine,* ca. 1930

James Henderson, *The End of Winter*

A. F. L. Kenderdine, *Homewards,* 1923

A. F. L. Kenderdine, *The Ferry Trail*

A. F. L. Kenderdine, *The Land of Promise,* 1923

C. W. Jefferys, *Saskatchewan River at Battleford,* 1924 or 1927

C. W. Jefferys, *The Valley of the Battle River, Saskatchewan,* 1930

Roland Gissing, *The Glen Ranch, Ghost River, Alberta*

Robert D. Symons, *Landscape Scene—Hills at Big Muddy*

L. L. FitzGerald, *Summer Afternoon, the Prairie,* 1921

L. L. FitzGerald, *Manitoba Landscape,* 1941

Illingworth Kerr, *Straw Stacks, March Thaw,* 1935

Illingworth Kerr, *Last Light, Boggy Creek Valley,* 1935

Illingworth Kerr, *Ernfold, Saskatchewan,* 1930

A. Y. Jackson, *Alberta Rhythm,* 1948

Robert Hurley, *Nocturne, 1933*

Robert Hurley, *Reflections,* ca. 1947

Robert Hurley, *After Harvest*, 1950

Robert Hurley, *Untitled, 1962*

Ernest Lindner, *Thunderstorm,* 1940s

Takao Tanabe, *The Land, #26, 1972*

Takao Tanabe, *The Land,* 4/75—East of Calgary, 1975

Otto Rogers, *Turning Cloud,* 1976

Otto Rogers, *Black Trees and Cube Sky,* 1971

Norman Yates, *Landscape Sixteen,* 1975

Norman Yates, *Landscape Thirty-Nine, 1979*

Robert Sinclair, *Cloudy Build-up,* 1973

Robert Sinclair, *Qu'Appelle, Sask. Sky,* 1973

Reta Cowley, *Farmstead near Hague,* 1969

Reta Cowley, *September Afternoon,* 1972

Dorothy Knowles, *Fields in Summer, 1969*

Dorothy Knowles, *Eagle Creek Valley, 1966*

Dorothy Martin, *The Old Fence,* ca. 1970

Ruth Pawson, *Fulfillment,* ca. 1952

Joe Acs, *Hague, Saskatchewan,* 1978

George Jenkins, *The Old Toal Place,* 1969

George Jenkins, *Prairie Pothole,* 1969

Wynona Mulcaster, *Winter Road,* 1971

Allen Sapp, *Little Bit Snowing,* 1983

Allen Sapp, *Man Chopping Some Wood,* 1983

Allen Sapp, *Getting Water from Slough,* 1983

Allen Sapp, *My Grandfather's Cows,* 1983

Eva Dennis, *Home Time at Capital Hill,* 1969

Jan Wyers, *These Good Old Thrashing Days,* 1957

Ann Harbuz, *Tom Geust's Store and Post Office,* 1976

William Kurelek, *Skating on Spring Run-Off,* 1974

William Kurelek, *A Bumper Harvest,* 1974

William Kurelek, *How Often at Night,* 1972

William Kurelek, *No Grass Grows on the Beaten Path* from *Fields,* copyright © 1976
William Kurelek, published by Tundra Books

ILLUSTRATION CREDITS

The author and publisher gratefully acknowledge permission to include illustrative material.

Joe Acs, *Hague, Saskatchewan*. Courtesy of the artist and Woltjen/Udell Gallery.

William Armstrong, *Buffalo Meat Drying, White Horse Plains, Red River* (C10502) and *A View of the Post Dog Trains leaving Fort Garry for St. Paul* (C10503). Courtesy of Public Archives Canada.

Reta Cowley, *Farmstead near Hague* and *September Afternoon*. Courtesy of the artist and Saskatchewan Arts Board.

Frank De Forest Schook, *Alberta Homesteader* and *Alberta Homesteader–After Four Years Effort*. Courtesy of Glenbow-Alberta Institute.

Eva Dennis, *Home Time at Capital Hill*. Courtesy of the artist and Saskatchewan Arts Board.

George E. Finlay, *Duck Hunters in Camp*. Courtesy of Glenbow Museum, Calgary, Alberta.

L. L. FitzGerald, *Summer Afternoon, Manitoba Landscape*, and *Landscape (Abstract)*. Courtesy of Patrick and Earl Green and Winnipeg Art Gallery. Photography by Ernest P. Mayer, The Winnipeg Art Gallery.

Charles Edwin Fripp, *The Dying North-West, The Graphic*, 31 August 1889 and *The New North-West, The Graphic*, 31 August 1889. Courtesy of Public Archives Canada.

Roland Gissing, *The Glen Ranch, Ghost River, Alberta*. Courtesy of Glenbow Museum, Calgary, Alberta.

S. P. Hall, *Pow-wow at Blackfoot Crossing* (C11068), [*Conference . . . at Blackfoot Crossing*] (C13070), *Sioux Buffalo Dance, The Graphic*, 19 November 1881. Courtesy of Public Archives Canada.

Ann Harbuz, *Tom Geust's Store and Post Office*. Courtesy of Victor Cicansky.

James Henderson, *The End of Winter*. Courtesy of The National Gallery of Canada, Ottawa. Gift of P. D. Ross, Ll.D., Ottawa, 1932. *Afternoon Sunshine* and *Winter Glory, Qu'Appelle Valley*. Photographs by Don Hall, A V Services, University of Regina. Courtesy of Norman Mackenzie Art Gallery.

W. G. R. Hind, *A Prairie Road* (C13967) *Settler's House and Red River Cart* (C13965) *Camping on the Plains* (C13974), and *Duck Hunting on the Prairies* (C13969). Courtesy of Public Archives Canada.

Robert Hurley, *Nocturne, Reflections, After Harvest*, and

Untitled. Courtesy of Western Producer Prairie Books.

A. Y. Jackson, *Alberta Rhythm*. Photograph by Larry Ostrom. Courtesy of the Art Gallery of Ontario.

C. W. Jefferys, *Saskatchewan River at Battleford*, (Private collection, Toronto) and *The Valley of the Battle River, Saskatchewan*. Dr. and Mrs. G. A. Fee, York Mills, Ontario. Courtesy of Robert Stacey.

George Jenkins, *The Old Toal Place* and *Prairie Pothole*. Photographs by Imagery Illustrations Ltd. Courtesy of the artist and Mendel Art Gallery.

Henri Julien, *NWMP Killing Ducks* and *The Sweet Grass Hills in Sight*. Courtesy of Glenbow-Alberta Institute.

Paul Kane, *The Man That Always Rides* and *Fort Edmonton*. Courtesy of Royal Ontario Museum, Toronto. *Fort Edmonton*. Courtesy of Stark Museum of Art, Orange, Texas. *A Prairie on Fire* and *Half Breeds Running Buffalo*. Courtesy of Royal Ontario Museum, Toronto.

A. F. L. Kenderdine, *Homewards*. Photograph by Don Hall, A V Services, University of Regina. Courtesy of Norman Mackenzie Art Gallery. *The Ferry Trail, North Saskatchewan River*. Courtesy of the National Gallery of Canada, Ottawa. *The Land of Promise*. Courtesy of Mrs. F. M. Beamish and the University of Saskatchewan.

Illingworth Kerr, *Ernfold, Saskatchewan* and *Last Light, Boggy Creek Valley*. Photographs by Imagery Illustrations Ltd., Saskatoon. Courtesy of the artist and Mendel Art Gallery. *Straw Stacks, March Thaw*. Courtesy of the artist and Glenbow-Alberta Institute.

Dorothy Knowles, *Fields in Summer*. Courtesy of the artist and Saskatchewan Arts Board. *Eagle Creek Valley*. Courtesy of the artist and the University of Saskatchewan.

William Kurelek, *How Often at Night*. Photograph by Creative Professional Photographers Ltd., Saskatoon. Courtesy of Mendel Art Gallery. *A Bumper Harvest* and *Skating on Spring Run-Off* from *Kurelek's Canada*. Courtesy of Pagurian Press. *No Grass Grows on the Beaten Path* from *Fields*, copyright © 1976 William Kurelek, published by Tundra Books.

Ernest Lindner, *Thunderstorm*. Courtesy of the artist and the University of Saskatchewan.

Washington Frank Lynn, *The Dakota Boat*, oil on canvas, 66.6 x 91.8 cm (donated by Mr. and Mrs.

Sam Cohen, G-71-94) and *The Forks*, oil on canvas, 61.0 x 86.6 cm. (donated by Mrs. J. K. Morton, G-70-7). Photographs by Ernest Mayer, The Winnipeg Art Gallery. Courtesy of the Winnipeg Art Gallery.

Dorothy Martin, *The Old Fence*. Courtesy of the artist and Saskatchewan Arts Board.

Wynona Mulcaster, *Winter Road*. Courtesy of the artist and the University of Saskatchewan.

Charles Adolphus Murray (Seventh Earl of Dunmore), *Souris River*. Courtesy of Glenbow Museum, Calgary, Alberta.

R. B. Nevitt, *On the March West* and *Fort Calgary in Summer*. Courtesy of Glenbow-Alberta Institute.

Ruth Pawson, *Fulfillment*. Courtesy of the artist and Saskatchewan Arts Board.

Peter Rindisbacher, *The Governor of Red River* (C1941) *A Souteaux Indian* (C1943) and *Winter Fishing* (C1932). Courtesy of Public Archives Canada.

Otto Rogers, *Turning Cloud*. Courtesy of the artist and Saskatchewan Arts Board. *Black Trees and Cube Sky*. Courtesy of the artist and the University of Saskatchewan.

Edward Roper, *Prairie Flowers* (C11036), *Breaking the Prairie* (C13884), and *A Settler's Home* (C11030). Courtesy of Public Archives Canada.

Allen Sapp, *Getting Water from Slough*, *Little Bit Snowing*, *Man Chopping Some Wood*, and *My Grandfather's Cows*. Courtesy of Allen Sapp Paintings, W. H. Baker, Vancouver, B.C.

F. B. Schell, *A Prairie Farmstead*, (C82967) *A Prairie Stream* (C82954), *The Harvester* (C82969), *A Mennonite Village* (C82983), and *The Virgin Prairie* (C82950). Courtesy of Public Archives Canada.

George Seton, *Bison Americanus* (C1055) and *Indian Dog Feast* (C1063). Courtesy of Public Archives Canada.

Inglis Sheldon-Williams, *After the Storm*, *The Landmark*, *The Fireguard*. Photographs by Don Hall, A V Services, University of Regina. Courtesy of the Norman Mackenzie Art Gallery. *The Fire Guardian*, *Threshing in Winter*, *Plowing the Fireguard*, and *Taking the Grain to Market* from *The Sphere*, 22 August 1903. Courtesy of Public Archives Canada.

Robert Sinclair, *Cloudy Build-up*. Courtesy of the artist and Glenbow-Alberta Institute. *Qu'Appelle Sask. Sky*. Courtesy of the artist and Edmonton Art Gallery.

Robert D. Symons, *Landscape Scene—Hills at Big Muddy*. Courtesy of Mrs. Hope Symons and the University of Saskatchewan.

Takao Tanabe, *The Land*, #26 (Photograph by Y. Boulerice) and *The Land, 4/75*. Courtesy of Canada Council Art Bank.

Frederick Verner, *Buffalo Grazing* and *Indians by Hut and Canoe*. Courtesy of Glenbow Museum, Calgary, Alberta.

Frederick Villiers, *Home for the First Year in the New West* from *The Graphic*, 9 November 1889 and *Lady Constance . . . "fixing" a War Dance* from *The Graphic*, 14 December 1889. Courtesy of Public Archives Canada.

H. J. Warre, *Buffalo Hunting* (C1624). Courtesy of Public Archives Canada.

Jan Wyers, *These Good Old Thrashing Days*. Photograph by Don Hall, A V Services, University of Regina. Courtesy of Norman Mackenzie Art Gallery.

Norman Yates, *Landscape Sixteen* and *Landscape Thirty-nine*. Courtesy of the artist and the Ring House Gallery, University of Alberta.

BIBLIOGRAPHY, BOOKS AND CATALOGUES

Ainslie, Patricia. *Inglis Sheldon-Williams.* Calgary: Glenbow-Alberta Institute, 1982.

Baker, Suzanne Devonshire. *Artists of Alberta.* Edmonton: University of Alberta, 1980.

Beauchamp, Elizabeth. *Norman Yates: Toward Landscape.* Edmonton: University of Alberta, 1983.

Bell, Michael J. *Image of Canada: Documentary watercolors and drawings from the permanent collection of the Public Archives of Canada.* Ottawa: Information Canada, 1972.

Bell, Michael J. *Painters in a New Land.* Toronto: McClelland and Stewart, 1973.

Bennett, John. *Northern Plainsmen.* Chicago: Aldine, 1969.

Bovey, Patricia and Ann Davis. *Lionel LeMoine Fitzgerald.* Winnipeg: Winnipeg Art Gallery, 1978.

Cavell, Edward, *Journeys to the Far West.* Toronto: James Lorimer, 1979.

Christie, Robert. *Watercolour Painting in Saskatchewan 1905-1980.* Saskatoon: Mendel Art Gallery, 1981.

Colgate, William. *Canadian Art, Its Origins and Development.* Toronto: Ryerson Press, 1979.

Davies, Evan, and Aled Vaughan. *Beyond the Old Bone Trail.* London: Cassells, 1960.

Donkin, John G. *Trooper and Redskin.* London: Sampson Low, 1889.

Eckhardt, Ferdinand. *150 Years of Art in Manitoba.* Winnipeg: Winnipeg Art Gallery, 1970.

Ediger, Eleanor P. *Western Landscape as History.* Ottawa: National Gallery of Canada, 1965.

Fenton, Terry. *Watercolour Painters from Saskatchewan.* Ottawa: National Gallery of Canada, 1971.

Frye, Northrop. *The Educated Imagination.* Toronto: CBC Publications, 1963.

Garland, Aileen. *Trails and Crossroads to Killarney.* Altona, Manitoba: D. W. Friesen, 1961.

Grant, George M. *Ocean to Ocean.* 1873; rpt. Edmonton: Hurtig, 1967.

Grant, George M. *Picturesque Canada.* Toronto: Beldon Bros., 1882.

Harper, J. Russell. *Painting in Canada: A History.* Toronto: University of Toronto Press, 1966.

Harper, J. Russell. *Paul Kane's Frontier.* Toronto: University of Toronto Press, 1971.

Harper, J. Russell. *William G. R. Hind.* Ottawa: National Gallery of Canada, 1976.

Harrison, Dick. *Unnamed Country: The Struggle for a Canadian Prairie Fiction.* Edmonton: University of Alberta, 1977.

Hedges, James B. *Building the Canadian West.* New York: MacMillan, 1939.

Hind, Henry Youle. *Narrative of the Canadian Red River Exploring Expedition of 1857.* London: Longman Green, 1860.

Hogarth, Paul. *Artists on Horseback: The Old West in Illustrated Journalism 1857-1900.* New York: Watson-Guptill Publications, 1972.

Honour, Hugh. *The New Golden Land: European Visions of America.* New York: Pantheon, 1976.

Huyda, Richard J. *Camera in the Interior 1858.* Toronto: The Coach House Press, 1975.

Josephy, Alvin M. *The Artist Was a Young Man: The Life Story of Peter Rindisbacher.* Fort Worth: Amon Carter Museum, 1970.

Kane, Paul. *Wanderings of an Artist among the Indians of North America.* Toronto: The Radisson Society of Canada, 1925.

Kline, Marcia B. *Beyond the Land Itself: Views of Nature in Canada and the United States.* Cambridge: Harvard University Press, 1970.

Kostash, Myrna. *All of Baba's Children.* Edmonton: Hurtig, 1977.

Kurelek, William. *Kurelek's Canada.* Toronto: Pagurian Press, 1978.

Lord, Barry. *A History of Painting in Canada: Toward a People's Art.* Toronto: NC Press, 1974.

Lorne, Marquis of. *Canadian Pictures.* London: Religious Tract Society, 1885.

Moppett, George. *Otto Rogers: A Survey 1973–1982.* Saskatoon: Mendel Art Gallery, 1982.

Muehlenbachs, Lelde. *Robert D. Symons.* Edmonton: Edmonton Art Gallery, 1974.

Nevitt, R. B., *A Winter at Fort Mcleod,* ed. Hugh E. Dempsey, Calgary: Glenbow-Alberta Institute and McClelland and Stewart West, 1974.

Owram, Doug. *Promise of Eden: The Canadian Expansionist Movement and the Idea of the West 1856–1900.* Toronto: University of Toronto Press, 1980.

Rees, Ronald. *Images of the Prairie.* Saskatoon: Mendel Art Gallery, 1979.

Reid, Dennis. *Alberta Rhythm.* Toronto: Art Gallery of Ontario, 1982.

Reid, Dennis. *A Concise History of Canadian Painting.* Toronto: Oxford University Press, 1974.

Render, Lorne. *The Mountains and the Sky.* Calgary: Glenbow-Alberta Institute and McClelland and Stewart West, 1974.

Robson, A. H. *Canadian Landscape Painters.* Toronto: Ryerson Press, 1932.

Roper, Edward. *By Track and Trail Through Canada.* London: W. H. Allen, 1891.

Smith, Bernard. *Place, Taste, Tradition, a Study of Australian Art since 1788.* Sydney: Ure Smith, 1945.

Stacey, Robert. *Charles William Jefferys, 1869-1951.* Kingston, Ontario: Agnes Etherington Art Centre, 1976.

Stegner, Wallace. *Wolf Willow.* New York: Viking Press, 1955.

Stevens, Peter. *Nothing But Spoons.* Montreal: Delta Canada, 1969.

Swanson, Jean. *Sky Painter.* Saskatoon: Western Producer Prairie Books, 1973.

Symons, Robert D. *Many Trails,* Toronto: Longmans, 1963.

Tennyson, Bertram. *The Land of Napoia.* Moosomin, NWT: Spectator Printing and Publishing Co., 1896.

Warre, Henry James. *Sketches in North America and the Oregon Territory.* London: Dickinson and Co., 1845.

Wilkin, Karen. *Art in Alberta: Paul Kane to the Present.* Edmonton: Edmonton Art Gallery, 1973.

Wilkin, Karen. *Painting in Alberta: An Historical Survey.* Edmonton: Art Gallery, 1980.

ESSAYS AND ARTICLES

Annett, Margaret T. "Paintings, Watercolours, Drawings, Frederick Arthur Verner." *Journal,* No. 20, Nov. 1976, National Gallery of Canada.

Ayre, Robert. "Lionel LeMoine Fitzgerald 1890-1956." *Canadian Art,* Autumn 1956.

Berry, Virginia. "Washington Frank Lynn: Artist and Journalist." *The Beaver,* Spring 1978.

Bovey, Patricia E. "Prairie Painting in the Dirty Thirties in Prairie Canada." In *The Dirty Thirties in Prairie Canada,* eds. D. Francis and H. Ganzevoort. Vancouver: Tantalus Research Ltd., 1980.

Brodsky, Anne Trueblood, et al. "Making a Home out of Existence: Nine Prairie Folk Artists," *Arts Canada,* Oct.-Nov., 1979.

Buchanan, Donald W. "A Prairie Approach to a Canadian Vision." *Canadian Art,* Jan.-Feb. 1963.

Chalmers, J. W. "Back and the Arctic." *North/Nord,* Vol. 19, May-June 1977.

Cook, Ramsay. "William Kurelek: A Prairie Boy's Visions." *Journal of Ukrainian Studies,* Vol. 5, No. 1, Spring 1980.

Dillow, Nancy E. "Inglis Sheldon-Williams." *Canadian Antiques Collector,* Vol. 8, No. 4, July-August 1973.

Evernden, Neil. "Beauty and Nothingness, Prairie as Failed Resource." *Landscape,* 27, March 1983.

Fenton, Terry. "High Culture in Prairie Canada," *ARTnews,* Vol. 8, No. 4, July-August 1973.

Ferguson, Ted. "Painting the West." *The Review,* No. 6, 1979.

Fry, Philip, "Prairie Space Drawings." *Arts Canada,* Early Autumn 1972.

Frye, Northrop. "Canadian and Colonial Painting." In *The Bush Garden: Essays on the Canadian Imagination.* Toronto: Anansi, 1971.

Harper, J. Russell. "William Hind and the Overlanders. *The Beaver,* Winter 1971.

Heath, Terrence. "Dorothy Knowles." *Arts Canada,* Early Autumn 1972.

Hood, Robert. "Some Account of the Cree and Other Indians, 1819. "*Alberta Historical Review,* Winter 1967.

Humphrys, Ruth. "Inglis Sheldon-Williams, Pioneer Artist of the Prairies." *The Beaver,* Winter 1979.

Kreisel, Henry. "The Prairie: A State of Mind." *Transactions of the Royal Society of Canada,* Series IV, vi, 1968.

McDermott, John Francis, "Peter Rindisbacher: Frontier Reporter." *Art Quarterly*, Spring 1949.

MacGregor, Reverend James, "Lord Lorne in Alberta." *Alberta Historical Review*, Spring 1964.

McLeod, Margaret Arnett. "Peter Rindisbacher, Red River Artist." *The Beaver*, December 1945.

Mandel, Eli. "Images of Prairie Man in A Region of the Mind." In *A Region of the Mind: Interpreting the Western Canadian Plains*, ed. Richard Allen. Regina: Canadian Plains Studies Centre, 1973.

Millard, Peter. "Reta Cowley: Fascinated by Gradual Changes." *ArtsWest*, May–June 1978.

Morton, W. L. "Seeing an Unliterary Landscape." *Mosaic* III, 3, 1970.

Murray, Joan. "Illingworth Kerr: The Theatre of Western Art." *Canadian Art Investors Guide*, Fall/Winter 1980.

Patton, Randolph. "Gus Kenderdine, Man, Artist, Teacher." *Green and White*, Fall 1954.

Rees, Ronald. "In a Strange Land: Homesick Pioneers on the Canadian Prairie." *Landscape*, 25,3, 1982.

Rees, Ronald. " 'Nostalgic Reaction' and the Canadian Prairie Landscape." *Great Plains Quarterly*, 2,3, 1982.

Rees, Ronald. "The Prairie: A Canadian Artist's View." *Landscape*, 21,2, 1977.

Sheldon-Williams, Inglis. "I was an Emigrant." Unpublished Manuscript, Glenbow-Alberta Institute, Calgary.

Shepard, Paul. "They Painted What They Saw." *Landscape*, 3,1, 1953.

Smith, Bernard. "Art and Environment in Australia." *Geographical Magazine*, 19,9, 1947.

Spry, Irene M. "Early Visitors to the Canadian Prairies." In *Images of the Plains: The Role of Human Nature in Settlement*, eds. B. W. Blouet and M. P. Lawson. Lincoln: University of Nebraska Press, 1974.

Stacey, Robert. "A Clear Northern Light." *Northward Journal*, No. 20, 1981.

Stacey, Robert. "Jefferys and the Toronto Art Students League 1888-1904." *Northward Journal*, No. 20, 1981.

Stanley, George F. G. "The Man Who Sketched The Great March." In *Men in Scarlet*, ed. Hugh Dempsey. Toronto: McClelland and Stewart, 1974.

Stanley, George F. G. "A Soldier at Fort Garry." *The Beaver*, Autumn 1957.

Stich, Klaus Peter. "Canada's Century, The Rhetoric of Propaganda," *Prairie Forum*, 1,1, 1976.

Todd, Ruthven. "The Imaginary Indian in Europe." *Art in America*, 60,4, 1972.

Warner, John Anson. "Allen Sapp." *ArtsWest*, September–October 1979.

Wasserman, Emily. "The Artist-Explorers." *Art in America*, 60,4, 1972.

Wilkin, Karen. "The Prairies: A Limited View." *Canadian Forum*, January 1975.

Wilson, Clifford. "Peter Rindisbacher, First Western Artist." *Canadian Art*, January–February 1963.

Wood, J. S. "James Henderson of the Qu'Appelle Valley." *Saskatchewan History*, 9,1, 1958.

Woodcock, George. "Possessing the Land." In *The Canadian Imagination: Dimensions of a Literary, Culture*, ed. David Staines. Cambridge: Harvard University Press, 1977.

Wright, Helen K. "An Interview with Illingworth Kerr, 1973." Unpublished Manuscript. Glenbow-Alberta Institute, Calgary.

INDEX